Living
the Lord's Prayer

Powerful & Relevant:
Unpacking Jesus' model prayer

DR DAVID CARR

RIVER
PUBLISHING

River Publishing & Media Ltd
Barham Court
Teston
Maidstone
Kent
ME18 5BZ
United Kingdom

info@river-publishing.co.uk

ISBN 978-1-908393-24-1
Printed in the United Kingdom

Contents

Introduction

As Christians we find ourselves living in a pluralistic society where very few people know anything of the Bible. This has not always been the case. I can vividly remember having to say The Lord's Prayer every day in school assembly in a hall full of my peers who, even now, would be able to recite it word for word. Whether they are walking with God or not, my contemporaries are likely to have these words of Jesus imprinted on their memory and hidden somewhere in their soul. They may even have spoken this same prayer at weddings, christenings, or in times of desperate anguish or loss.

Sadly, these days are all but gone. The Lord's Prayer has been replaced by alternative expressions of corporate worship and reflection, which are designed to keep everyone happy and maintain an uneasy truce between the many systems of belief within our society. Loving our neighbour, as we are told to do in Scripture, has all too often become a license to settle for the lowest common denominator, and we are now, I believe, reaping the consequences of all we have pushed aside.

The truth is that the Lord's Prayer is revolutionary! Contained within it is everything that society needs to connect with the God of the universe who made humanity in His image. Opening out before us is a road on which we will journey together through this prayer into a deeper intimacy with the God who provides, sustains, protects and guides. As you read each chapter I pray you will meet the Father, whose power is unlimited, whose tenderness is deeper than any other, and whose protection is guaranteed, regardless of whatever life throws at you.

1. The Fatherhood of God

Lord, Teach us to pray

Now it came to pass, as He was praying in a certain place, when He ceased, that one of His disciples said to Him, 'Lord, teach us to pray, as John also taught his disciples.

Luke 11:1

The Lord's Prayer is recorded in two of the four Gospels: Matthew and Luke. In both accounts, the context is about the importance of personal and intimate prayer in our walk with God. In Matthew, Jesus is teaching the multitudes about prayer during the Sermon on the Mount, but it is in Luke's gospel that Jesus was prompted to give a response to the question from one of the disciples, "teach us to pray." We are not told who asked the question, but it was obviously asked on behalf of the whole group.

Notice that it was much more than a request for a set of set words to be recited as a ritual, "Give us a prayer to pray." These men wanted to learn how to pray: it was a plea for increased connection to God the Father through Jesus. They had watched Jesus pray to His Father in ways that were radically different from anything they had ever seen or experienced, and they wanted some of that for themselves!

How prayer used to happen

The twelve disciples were ordinary men who had grown up in the Jewish tradition where the High Priest interceded on their behalf. Once a year wearing full regalia, he would enter the Holy of Holies to meet with God who was infinite, remote and far too holy to be approached by the average Jew. Any connection to God required a go-between: intimacy with God for the individual was not part of the deal.

In the Old Testament, the book of Exodus tells of how the people of Israel were called out of Egypt to eventually settle in their own land called Cannan. By introducing religious ritual and ceremony God further set them apart as His own people and intricate laws were established in order to give Israel its identity. Priests were there to pray to Yahweh on behalf of the people, and they were given special instructions as to how to carry out their role.

Every now and then, there would be people in the Old Testament who broke away from the set rituals to access God directly. King David was a man who pointed the way towards how it would be when Jesus came. He didn't need anyone to teach him how to pray, for God had been close to him when he was just a shepherd boy in the fields with only sheep for company. When he became king, and for all the years up to his death, he maintained the same intimacy with God which was poured out in worship, dance, song and poetry. For David, God was always accessible, always available.

Blessed is the man You choose,
And cause to approach You,
That he may dwell in Your courts.
We shall be satisfied with the goodness of Your house,
Of Your holy temple.

Psalm 65:4

David's relationship with God echoed through the following centuries until the coming of Jesus when this revolutionary way of relating to God was finally available to all.

Since then, history has taught us that it's been an ongoing struggle for the common man to access God for himself. History tells us how it was perfectly normal for congregations to turn up at church, to hear the choir sing, listen to the Bible read in Latin so it couldn't be understood, and hear the priest preach on whatever he wanted to because no one could stop him! People had to sit there in their pews unable to participate in any way other than when they were told to. Prayers were said from the front and a corporate "amen" was the sum total of a person's agreement in worship.

The prayer that Jesus taught us to pray is available for everyone. It has always meant to be a guide for a life of intimacy in prayer with our Heavenly Father. When the disciples asked Jesus to teach them how to pray, he wasn't aloof or mysterious about it; He didn't talk about high priests and hierarchy having to stand in the gap. Everyone is invited to pray it and call God "Father" wherever they are in life, from the youngest to the oldest, male or female, believer or non-believer. So as we start this journey together, let's ask, "Lord, teach us to pray."

Our Father in heaven,
Hallowed be Your name.
Your kingdom come.
Your will be done
On earth as it is in heaven.
Give us this day our daily bread.
And forgive us our debts,
As we forgive our debtors.
And do not lead us into temptation,
But deliver us from the evil one.
For Yours is the kingdom and the power and the glory forever.
Amen.
Matthew 6:9-13

"Our Father"

You, O Lord, are our Father; Our Redeemer from Everlasting is Your
name. Isaiah 63:16b

What is a good father like?

Many people find this question impossible to answer because their experience of "father" has been a bad one. Instead of knowing unconditional love, provision, protection, forgiveness, fairness, covering and kindness, they experience judgement, harshness, absence, threat and neglect. Our society is reeling from the pain of fatherlessness and confused by the lie that one-parent families give as secure a foundation as those with two. Politicians try their best to paper over the cracks by passing laws to protect the vulnerable — and I'm glad they do — but until we acknowledge that at the heart of the issue is the need in every man, woman and child to find out who they really are in God, we will always be struggling to keep our heads above water.

For some of us, even saying "Our Father" is enough to send us running away. When we have had a bad experience of an earthly father, we tend to see God through that filter. In other words, we see God according to our cognitive default. The flip side is that if we have had a great earthly father, we think God is just the same as Dad. But the reverse is true: our earthly Dad is an echo of our Heavenly Dad.

I once talked with a 35 year-old woman about how her father sexually abused her between the ages of 6 and 16.

I remember thinking, "Wow, how is she ever going to be able to associate fatherhood with anything other than the vilest pit of resentment?"

I am aware of others who have been abused by priest fathers who can never hope to be set free from the effects of the abuse by their own efforts.

The truth is, it's only when we receive supernatural revelation and truth from God that we can get over our cognitive default setting. When God changes the heart, He renews the mind.

For some people "Our Father" is a cry of the heart to be taken from loneliness to belonging, from sadness to joy, from pain to healing. In two simple words, Jesus turns tradition upside down and invites those who feel outside the camp to enter all the way in and embrace One who is the perfect embodiment of fatherhood. For others, it is an acknowledgment of what they already know God to be in their lives and offers comfort and security. Whatever the emotion connected to "Our Father" isn't it wonderful that Jesus invited us to call His own Father our Father too?

So what is our Father like?

Our Father is relational
I'm so glad that Christianity is about relationship, not religion.

The Bible says,

That which we have seen and heard we declare to you, that you also may have fellowship with us; and truly our fellowship is with the Father and with His Son Jesus Christ. 1 John 1:3.

I have already said how it has often been the way that over the centuries priests and clergy have prevented the ordinary members of their congregation from having access to God for themselves. It is not only in Christianity and Judaism that this hierarchical structure happens though. In Islam, for instance, when a particular embroidery has been completed, it will always have a stitch missed out so that the garment is not perfect. This reflects how it is only God who is perfect, so nothing else can be.

But can't God be perfect and relational at the same time?

Why would God send His only Son into the world as a baby only to be crucified and resurrected if He didn't want to reach out to us and draw us into a love that the world cannot offer?

There is no other God like ours! He was prepared to send His Son Jesus in order that He could experience the essence of what it is to be human. No other God in any other religion has ever stooped so low in order to identify with His people.

For you know the grace of our Lord Jesus Christ, that though He was rich, yet for your sakes He became poor, that you through His poverty might become rich. 2 Corinthians 8:9

When we address God as "Our Father" we are invited into a father-child relationship. Not only that, but we know that He understands and empathises with us because He has, through Jesus, experienced everything that life can ever or will ever throw at us. Psalm 103:14 says, *"For He knows our frame."* Our Father is not remote; He is very near and welcomes us to come closer as we pray. God has designed us to be in relationship with Him and when the relationship breaks down for any reason, He works hard to repair it as any good parent would.

When the disciples asked Jesus how to pray, they were suddenly elevated into the heavenly places and given complete access to the fullness of God's household. A complete inheritance waited for them on the day of Pentecost when they would be filled with the Holy Spirit, adding a robe of righteousness to the ring of sonship they were given that day when talking with Jesus. It signified a new level of relationship, not characterised by religion, but by intimacy and love.

When a couple legally adopts a child, that child is given full access to everything it means to be a part of the family. When Jesus tells the disciples to call God "Our Father" He is giving them access to all the rights and privileges on offer for being a child of God. The Bible puts it this way,

Just as He chose us in Him before the foundation of the world, that we should be holy and without blame before Him in love, having predestined us to adoption as sons by Jesus Christ to Himself, according to the good pleasure of His will, to the praise of the glory of His grace, by which He made us accepted in the Beloved. Ephesians 1:4-6

Not only that but our family has a name! God is so wonderfully relational that He is prepared to put His Name to us, to give us a secure identity and to offer us the ultimate protection.

For this reason I bow my knees to the Father of our Lord Jesus Christ, from whom the whole family in heaven and earth is named. Ephesians 1:14-15

Isn't it amazing to think that we are related to someone so magnificently perfect and yet loved so completely, no matter what?

Our Father provides

One of the worst punishments you can give a man or a woman is to put them in solitary confinement. Human beings were not meant to be alone, and from the beginning of Genesis when God gives Adam a helper called Eve, the Bible is full of the truth that an important facet of God's Fatherhood is that of provider. Throughout the Bible there are stories of God providing food and water in deserts, rain in drought and a pillar of fire and a cloud to show the way. He gives children to the barren, companions for the lonely, sleep to the restless, beauty for ashes and gladness instead of sadness. He sends birds to feed the hungry, pours oil into empty jars, and speaks calm into dangerous storms.

God is actively providing for each of His children day by day and when we simply pray "Our Father" we can be comforted to know that He is there as the One who will supply all we need to live life as He intended us to live it.

If a son asks for bread from any father among you, will he give him a stone? Or if he asks for a fish, will he give him a serpent instead of a fish? Or if he asks for an egg, will he offer him a scorpion? If you then, being evil, know how to give good gifts to your children, how much more will your heavenly Father give the Holy Spirit to those who ask Him! Luke 11:11-13

Our Father protects

You are my hiding place;
You shall preserve me from trouble;
You shall surround me with songs of deliverance.
Psalm 32:7

When David was a shepherd his job was obviously to protect the sheep in his care. We know from 1 Samuel 17 that he killed both a lion and a bear who had posed a threat to his flock and by writing these words, David acknowledges how, in turn, God is his protector.

Good fathers protect their children. When we are brought into the family of God we come under His protection and care. He is the Almighty God who created the heavens and the earth, yes, but he is also "Abba" or "Daddy" to whom we can run when we are in danger.

Our Father is watchful

Not only does Father protect us when we are in sudden danger, He watches over us all the time.

The Lord himself watches over you! The Lord stands beside you as your protective shade. Psalm 121:5 NLT

Growing up, I had a Dad who I loved dearly amongst all men and when he died, I remember coming to realize the enormity of no longer having a Dad who was there to be what I needed him to be. The same happened when I lost my spiritual Dad.

God spoke to me and told me that I couldn't have a Dad all my life so I would just have to go out and become one! And then He told me that He had always been my Father and always would be. You can't get much better than that! I get so excited about it! My "Abba", my "Daddy", is always with me, always watching over me and always protecting me when there is no one left in that earthly role. Won't you be encouraged that Father is the same for you today and always?

Our Father is accessible

So many children are growing up with fathers who are too busy to spend time with them. Society has moved to a place where the family unit has become vulnerable to the pressure of the economic climate, meaning both parents often have to get paid jobs. Also, many fathers are absent from their children's lives by choice or circumstance, which makes children grow up without access to any male role model. A fatherless child, even one loved deeply by the rest of the family, will always have a missing link in its life, one way or another.

We all need Dads.

When the disciples asked Jesus to teach them to pray, it was a cry not of ignorance or immaturity, but one of desperation for closeness to God in comparison to the experiences of their forefathers. They had been emotionally and religiously blown away by how Jesus openly referred to Almighty God as "Father" throughout His ministry. There was a purity, simplicity and accessibility in His relationship as Son to Father that appealed to their deepest needs.

In the Garden of Gethsemane, when Jesus was at His wits end, in overwhelming anguish, stress and pain, He cried out,

Abba, Father, all things are possible for You. Take this cup away from Me; nevertheless, not what I will, but what You will. (Mark 14:36

"Abba" is literally translated as "Daddy" and when Jesus uses this word, it shows that even in the most desperate of circumstances He was able to access His Father without any preamble. Father was right there with Him.

Our Father is closer than we know and always ready to hear us, whatever our circumstance and however we are feeling. He is totally accessible.

Our Father is fair

My Dad never smacked me because he was the type of man you respected and, in the right sense, feared. I knew that if ever he floored me, I would struggle to get up again as he was very strong.

But he never did, and I was comforted by the fact that the same power that could have taken me out, was the same power that protected me as a frightened little boy. It's just the same with God. He could destroy me, but in truth He will never behave in any way that is in conflict with His loving nature and His love for me. My Father is always fair and I am never in danger, even though He is very, very powerful.

Do you remember the saying, "Wait until your father gets home"? It is sometimes used by mothers unable to cope with their wayward children. Weary and worn out, they use the mention of Dad coming home as a threat. I understand that children can be hard work, but in reality, the fairer route would be for Mum to deal with the misdemeanors there and then so that Dad is not seen as the one to fear!

When I go to my Father to pray and I need correction or discipline, He always deals with my issues there and then, loving me through them, leading me to face what I need to, in order to get me back on track. He is a loving disciplinarian when we need it, and we should not be afraid to approach Him because very often, love is actually experienced through correction.

For the Lord disciplines the one He loves, and chastises every son whom He receives. Hebrews 12:6 ESV

Our Father is neither male nor female

I want to make it clear that The Lord's Prayer is not about the sexuality of God. God the Father is not a man, He is Spirit.

God is Spirit, and those who worship Him must worship in spirit and truth. John 4:24

When we pray "Our Father" we are not praying to a man but to a being far greater in a realm far beyond our understanding where there is no gender. Male and female gender is part of our earthly condition, which is reinforced by the fact that in heaven, as in Christ, there will be no "male and female" (Galatians 3:28). God is not half-man and half-woman; He is not bi-sexual. The Bible contains references to His fathering and His mothering because as Spirit, He embraces everything a man and woman are. We can be confident when we pray "Our Father" that within that title is the richness of male and female meaning that He understands whatever is prayed by both men and women. There is no gender bias, no favouritism in our God.

The title of "Father" given here in The Lord's Prayer is one of position and function rather than gender. God has labelled Himself "Father" with its inevitable masculine associations in order that we might be able to understand His function and position. The male is the giver of life whereas the female is the cultivator and receiver of life. So in His description as Father, God, being a giving God, adopts the foundational role of Father. It is the Spirit that bears witness to the fact that we are God's children.

For as many as are led by the Spirit of God, these are sons of God. For you did not receive the spirit of bondage again to fear, but you received the Spirit of adoption by whom we cry out, 'Abba, Father.' The Spirit Himself bears witness with our spirit that we are children of God. Romans 8:14-16

In other words, I can't prove He's my Dad but I just know He's my Dad. Something inside me knows that the Spirit who is in me, is the same Spirit in Jesus when He cried out "Abba Father" in Gethsemane. My adoption as a child of God has brought me into an experience beyond my understanding – that I am totally protected in my Father's love.

The Father of all fathers

"For as the body is clad in the cloth, and the flesh in the skin, and the bones in the flesh and the heart in the bulk, so are we soul and body clad and enclosed in the goodness of God: yea and more homelie, for all they vanish and waste away, the goodness of God is ever whole and more near to us without any comparison." (Julian of Norwich 1342-c1416, Sixteen Revelations of Divine Love)

These words were written many centuries ago by the English mystic, Dame Julian of Norwich. The truths within it are as real today as they were then, that as God's children we are completely enclosed by His Fatherly goodness. Whatever our experiences of our own father, we are defined by a spiritual relationship that supersedes any of our earthly relationships.

God really is our Father and we really are His children. That's good news!

I love that these two simple words at the opening of the prayer Jesus taught us to pray, contain infinite richness and depth. Let's not skim over them next time. Let's pause to think about our Father who loved us enough to endure separation from His own Son so that we can be free.

- What has been your experience of "father"?
- Is he absent from your life? Did he leave you? Has he passed away?
- Has he been a good or bad, weak or strong Dad?
- Have you judged your Dad for his weaknesses and failings?
- Do you thank your heavenly Father for your earthly father often enough?

The time will come, if it hasn't already, when our earthly fathers will pass away. What then? Who will cover us, protect us, and care for us when we need it most? To whom can we look for our identity and value? Who will be our defender and speak out words of justice on our behalf? Only God, our true Father.

Meditate

Our Father has no grandchildren: He is Father to all. Throughout our lives from birth to death He is our protector, defender, guide, friend, confidante and comfort. He will discipline us, love us fiercely and watch over us until we finally end our days on earth, and then we will be with Him throughout eternity.

When all else has failed us, when natural strength diminishes and the grave calls to the outer man 'your day is near;' when the trappings of this age become only beacons of human achievements; when the past has more memories than the future has opportunities, then what rests in the inner man is of more value than treasures of gold. When sight is limited and hearing restricted, then the music of the heart and the dance of the soul become the entertainment of our being. And all that we have belonged to has either grown into its own world of busyness or departed to the garden of purity before us; then as seniors the reality of His eternal Fatherhood dispels the fear of frailty in human loneliness. Locked by human longevity or physical weakness we will never diminish the heart's cry by the Spirit of Jesus, 'Abba, Father, remember me.' He will not leave you comfortless or alone: it is not good to be alone. 'Come home,' He will say, 'to Father's house. A room especially prepared for you.'

Thank you Abba, my Daddy. Thank you.

2. The Rule of Heaven

Who is in Heaven?

The Nicene Creed is one of the oldest documents of faith, which refers to Heaven as the place God created:

I believe in one God the Father Almighty,

Maker of heaven and earth,

And of all things visible and invisible:

And in one Lord Jesus Christ, the only-begotten Son of God,

Begotten of his Father before all worlds,

God of God, Light of Light,

Very God of very God,

Begotten, not made,

Being of one substance with the Father,

By whom all things were made;

Who for us men, and for our salvation came down from heaven,

And was incarnate by the Holy Ghost of the Virgin Mary,

And was made man,

And was crucified also for us under Pontius Pilate.

He suffered and was buried,

And the third day he rose again according to the Scriptures,

And ascended into heaven,

And sitteth on the right hand of the Father.

And he shall come again with glory to judge both the quick and the dead:

Whose kingdom shall have no end.

And I believe in the Holy Ghost,

The Lord and giver of life,

Who proceedeth from the Father and the Son,

Who with the Father and the Son together is worshipped and glorified,

Who spake by the Prophets.

And I believe one Catholick and Apostolick Church.

I acknowledge one Baptism for the remission of sins.

And I look for the Resurrection of the dead,

And the life of the world to come.

Amen.

(The Book of Common Prayer 1662)

When Jesus instructs His disciples to pray, He begins with "Our Father" and follows this with "...in Heaven" (Matthew 6:9) to show them both how they should approach God and, in addressing him, where He is.

Although the Bible tells us that God can never and will never be contained in any one place...

But who is able to build Him a temple, since heaven and the heaven of heavens cannot contain Him... 2 Chronicles 2:6

...we also know that it is from Heaven that God rules and reigns supreme and to where, when we acknowledge Him as Lord of our life, we will one day go.

For our citizenship is in heaven, from which we also eagerly wait for the Saviour, the Lord Jesus Christ, who will transform our lowly body that it may be conformed to His glorious body, according to the working by which He is able even to subdue all things to Himself. Philippians 3: 20-21

I'm so glad I know where I'm going when I leave this earth, aren't you?

So where is Heaven?

Over the centuries, scholars and religious leaders have tried to define where Heaven is located and what it's like, but the truth is, we don't really know.

What we can be sure of though, is that it isn't an extension of the natural universe. Heaven can't be seen or entered via sight or cognitive perception. We only "see" it by faith.

When the Russian cosmonaut, Yuri Gagarin became the first human being to journey into outer space, he was reported to have said, "I don't see any God up here." However, it is now accepted that the atheist Russian President Nikita Khrushchev was the one who actually invented these words, accrediting them to Gagarin in an attempt to disprove the existence of God for propaganda purposes. In reality, the cosmonaut was said to be an Orthodox Christian who baptised his daughter the day before embarking on his journey. Gagarin would have known God could never be "seen" during a space flight.

A lot of what has fuelled the study and debate on the whereabouts of Heaven has come from what the Bible says about it, but there are some streams of thought that are pure speculation. It all gets very confusing and serious tensions have always existed between different groups of people who all think that their view is the right one.

In the second century, a Christian bishop called Papias taught that Heaven existed in three levels: Heaven itself, Paradise and the City, which I think is a fair description as we consider the second section of The Lord's Prayer – although I will slightly vary the Bishop's views as we go along.

But before we do any of that, we should very briefly explore how the three main bodies of Christendom understand Heaven in order to grasp our history a bit better.

How Orthodox Christians understand Heaven

After the split between the Orthodox Christians and the Roman Catholics in the 11th Century over the issues to do with the creed, Constantinople was established as the centre of Christian Orthodoxy. It was from here that a theology of Heaven emerged similar to that of Bishop Papias centuries before.

The Orthodox Christian believes that the lowest level of Heaven is Paradise, which at the point of creation touched earth and which was sinless until Adam and Eve chose to spoil it by giving way to temptation and eating of the Tree of The Knowledge of Good and Evil. After the fall of man, that "link" was severed from the earth, making it impossible for a man or woman to enter back into Paradise other than through an encounter with Christ.

The Orthodox view states that when Jesus died on the cross, an "entrance" into Paradise was reinstated and everyone who would freely confess His sacrifice could reconnect with it, as happened with the thief at Golgotha:

Then he said to Jesus, 'Lord, remember me when You come into Your kingdom.' And Jesus said to him, 'Assuredly, I say to you, today you will be with Me in Paradise.' Luke 23:42-43

Today, Orthodox Christians view Heaven as a place of green pastures; a place of light and repose where all sickness, sighing and sorrow flee away. It is only God who has the final say over who enters Heaven where man, upon death, is free to relate to God as Triune – Father, Son and Holy Spirit for eternity.

How Roman Catholics understand Heaven

In Catholicism, Heaven is a place of supreme happiness, a blessed community of all people who are perfectly incorporated into Christ and who will never again live in darkness.

There shall be no night there: they need no lamp nor light of the sun, for the Lord God gives them light. And they shall reign forever and ever. Revelation 22:5

Rather than being a geographical place, like Australia or Bermuda, Catholics believe that Heaven is a state of relational fellowship in Beatific Vision with the Almighty, where the soul is free to contemplate the wonder of God following the intermediate stage of Purgatory (a place of temporary punishment to cleanse those people destined for Heaven).

Pope John Paul the Second said that Heaven is, "...our meeting with the Father which takes place in the Risen Christ through the communion of the Holy Spirit."

How Protestants understand Heaven

There's not much I can say here because they don't seem to be able to agree!

In Protestantism, there is not one universally accepted view on Heaven, which is made all the more complicated by the fact that the 32,900 denominations all have their own specific theological interpretations of it!

What I can say, however, is that on the fundamental issues there is agreement that Heaven is the place from which God rules, reigns and exercises His authority.

And I heard a loud voice from heaven saying, 'Behold, the tabernacle of God is with men, and He will dwell with them, and they shall be His people. God Himself will be with them and be their God.' Revelation 21:3

For Protestants, Heaven is a place where, though the work of the cross, there is no longer a separation between man and God, which means that we are offered eternal and complete union with Father, Son and Holy Spirit.

At this point, I could digress into teaching about post-, pre- or ante-millennialism or start to unpack the theology of Calvinism and Arminianism, but that is not for this book. Maybe I'll save that for some other time!

It's all very well understanding our theological history, but what is our own experience of Heaven? Do we have to wait until we die to experience it or does God give us glimpses of what it is like while we are alive on earth? If so, does that mean that situations and circumstances can change to reflect the characteristics of Heaven and the reign of God there?

I think we know the answer to that, don't we?

A few years ago, Pope Benedict 16th said,

"The blessing hands of Christ are like a roof that protects us. But at the same time, they are a gesture of opening up, tearing the world open so that Heaven may enter in, may become 'present' within it."

The truth is that while we can't see Heaven – and while we are alive on earth we can't live there eternally – God doesn't reserve the blessings housed in Heaven just for when we die. The wonderful, heavenly presence of God can positively affect our lives and the lives of those around us, both inside and outside of the church.

The time I went to Heaven

So far, I have visited heaven twice in my lifetime.

One of those occasions was in 1994 when I had just left a career in football and entered into full time ministry. This was the year I took fifty men away to Cliff College for a weekend of relaxation with God and each other. We arrived on the Friday evening and after we had unpacked and settled in a bit, we all met up in the double glazed meeting room for a time of worship led by Tony on keyboards and Phil on guitar. Good times!

Within minutes of starting worship, we could feel the presence of God enter the room. It was fantastic. At some point during the singing I began to feel very faint and started keeling over. I felt similar to the way one would feel being given an old fashioned anaesthetic, where you had to breathe through a rubber mask designed to gradually put you to sleep. I could hear people singing and the instruments playing, but everything sounded like a muffled echo, gradually getting further and further away as I drifted off.

It soon dawned on me, however, that instead of being asleep, I was in Heaven. I don't know whether I was there in the spirit or whether the spirit came down on me, but I tell you, what I experienced next is still as clear as a bell in my memory, as if it happened just yesterday.

I remember standing at the side of the throne of God. I couldn't see His face and I didn't hear Him speak, and yet I "heard" Him speak. He never spoke, but He spoke! What I mean is, just as we "hear" God by conviction or through prophetic utterance, we hear Him not as a voice as we would hear in an earthly sense, but in our knower. We know we have heard Him in our knower.

God asked me what I saw. I told Him I saw thousands of knights in armour with shields and emblems, drinking, laughing and making merry while propping each other up. He told me that this was a picture of His Church at the time – oblivious to the battle, focussed on having a good time and preoccupied with each other. He went on to tell me all the things that were going to happen in the UK, who the next Prime Minister was going to be, and how our nation would be brought to its knees by recession. God asked me if I was prepared to go to prison for Him and I asked Him about the issue of homosexuality. He told me that I would be attacked for my decision not to marry single gender couples, telling me that this was an attack on His creation.

I was warned to tell no one what I had been shown, but He would send ministers to me who would know that I had been given fresh prophetic insight from Heaven. This did happen over the next six months as leaders from all over the UK came saying they knew God had told me something important.

After God had finished speaking, just as I had been drawn into Heaven, I was drawn back into the natural, sucked into my body again, to find everyone in the room had been taken-out by the Spirit of God. I saw grown men draped over chairs, weeping under the influence of the Holy Spirit; no one was left standing. The fear of God hit me for the first time and I ran to my room, laying in darkness as I felt so unclean and unworthy to have been in His presence. My friends found me eventually, shaking under the fear and conviction of the Lord, sober at the thought of what the months and years ahead would unfold. And sure enough, all that God had spoken came true.

The following morning at breakfast, the caretaker of the site came up to me and said, "Reverend Carr, I just want to say it was incredible last night. We have 150 freshers from Hull University Christian Union staying here and they had a head-banging Gospel concert, which was so loud I thought they would disturb you. But even through the double glazing in your meeting room, all I could hear was the beautiful sound of your male voice choir drowning out the campus!" Confused, I told him we had no male voice choir, just fifty men, a keyboard and a guitar. He said "Stop teasing me! I've never heard singing like it!"

It was then I realised we had had an angelic visitation of a male voices joining in with us as we touched Heaven and Heaven touched us.

Amazing!

Isn't God wonderful?

So you can't see it, touch it or hear it in the natural, but Heaven is closer than we know. In the gospel of Matthew Jesus says,

Repent, for the kingdom of heaven is at hand. Matthew 3:2 ESV

Heaven exists. I've been there! I don't doubt it for one second.

Paul's experience

Just as I am not sure what really happened to me on that day in 1994, the apostle Paul seems to have had a similar experience of Heaven. In 2 Corinthians 12:2 he is widely accepted to be writing about his experience on the road to Damascus:

I know a man in Christ who fourteen years ago—whether in the body I do not know, or whether out of the body I do not know, God knows—such a one was caught up to the third heaven.

So what on earth is the third Heaven? What are the first and second Heavens?

And where are they?

It is a strange concept for us to grasp today as we are not used to the traditions and teachings around in the days of Paul, but I want to help us understand this in a little more detail if we can, in order that it will lead us into a fresh revelation of God and His ways.

The first Heaven

This describes the physical world – the world in which we live and the world that declares His handiwork.

The heavens declare the glory of God; And the firmament shows His handiwork. Psalm 19:1

I went to New Zealand once and was amazed by how little pollution there is over there. One night I looked up at the sky and I couldn't believe how many stars there were. It was like above me was a blanket of tiny pinpricks of light as far as the eye could see! This is the how the heavens declare the glory of God for us all to see and to remember that He is far greater than anything in creation, as He is the creator of all of it.

The second Heaven

Another name for the second Heaven is "the heavenlies" which is used in the Bible to describe the realm of spiritual activity and authority into which God has,

...raised us up together, and made us sit together in the heavenly places in Christ Jesus, that in the ages to come He might show the exceeding riches of His grace in His kindness toward us in Christ Jesus. Ephesians 2:6-7

This is the area of the supernatural, a place where the enemy rules. Satan was thrown out from Heaven and established his rule in the heavenlies. It is from here that battles are fought and wars rage.

When an aeroplane flies higher and higher through cloud, it will eventually reach a place where the skies are clear and the sun shines bright. In effect, the sun has never gone away, it has just been blocked out by cloud. It's the same with spiritual things. God never goes away, He is always present, but there is a realm of dark cloud that can obscure our view of Him until He breaks through, or we break through, and things become clearer and lighter. Remember, demonic forces are intent on blocking our view of our Father.

How many of us have walked away before God breaks through, because we are tired of trying to make things work? In the book of Daniel we read how when Daniel prayed for a revelation of the Son and didn't get it quickly enough, he walked away, only to be met by the warring angel, Michael, who had been battling with the King of Persia on Daniel's behalf. Michael told him it was inevitable that he would win the battle, but it had not been easy and by the time he had got through, Daniel had walked off!

Battles in the heavenlies are going on all the time and God sends His angels to fight on our behalf. But not only that, we have been given every authority over the principalities and powers to overcome whatever the enemy throws at us, so we mustn't give up or walk away, even if victory is a long time coming, or even if the outcome is not as we had hoped. God will make everything complete in its time.

For we do not wrestle against flesh and blood, but against principalities, against powers, against the rulers of the darkness of this age, against spiritual hosts of wickedness in the heavenly places. Ephesians 6:11-13

Let me be clear: Heaven is our home and the place we will eventually come to rest if our lives belong to Jesus. But we do not spend our lives simply waiting for Heaven. No! You and I have been given a seat in heavenly places and God has given us all authority in this spiritual war to fight and win. If I am given a seat in the House of Lords, it is a privilege and an honour and I take up the seat reserved for me, otherwise it will remain empty and unused. In the same way, when I encounter evil of any kind, whether it is sickness or sin, I rise up and take my seat as an elected member of God's house in His authority and His strength. Not only that, I receive the blessings available to me as a child of my Father.

Thank you, Father, for equipping us with all power and authority to stand firm and not allow the clouds to block out the sun.

Blessed be the God and Father of our Lord Jesus Christ, who has blessed us with every spiritual blessing in the heavenly places in Christ. Ephesians 1:3

The third Heaven

The Lord's Prayer identifies, "Our Father, who is in heaven." Our Father rules and reigns in all realms, but He has established His residence in Heaven or the Third Heaven. In Matthew 6:14 Jesus tells the crowd that if they forgive one another, their Heavenly Father will also forgive them. Jesus is reinforcing that forgiveness is only truly valuable when it has been authorised by Heaven. In other words, Heaven is the place of authority.

Let me explain.

I am often racing around like there is no tomorrow. I can be up early for meetings at one end of the country one day, only to find that the next day I am due at the opposite end of the country. My diary will tell me I have a study day booked one day and the following day I will be checking in at an airport ready to fly across the Atlantic. Life is never boring I can tell you!

Regardless of where I find myself, I know that my centre of operations, my place of authority, rests in one place: my office. It is where my emails get answered, phone calls taken and where all my "stuff" is. My secretary is based there to keep things running smoothly and make sure nothing gets missed. So while I am out and about, I can rest secure that I have a place identified as the hub of my ministry.

In the same way, God positions Himself in Heaven as the place of His authority and permanence. There will be no passing away of Heaven; there is no danger of God being overthrown by the enemy there. It is purely His place of operation, where His rule and reign is authorised and from where He authorises His perfect will and desire.

As we saw in chapter one, God has no body, He is Spirit, and as such, He is not confined to Heaven, Earth or anywhere else. But with 531 references to Heaven in the Bible, it is clear that it's important to God that He communicates the importance of it.

Because it is the place God lives in, there is no strife or ugliness, but only beauty and majesty. Blessings are sent from Heaven:

Bring all the tithes into the storehouse, that there may be food in My house, and try Me now in this,' says the Lord of hosts, 'If I will not open for you the windows of heaven and pour out for you such blessing that there will not be room enough to receive it. Malachi 3:10

And in Revelation, John writes of his visions of gold, amethysts, trees, rivers of life, angelic hosts and astounding beauty.

Heaven is a place in which God has prepared a place for us and one day we will live there with Him, free from anxiety and fear, pain and loss; fully complete. Matthew Henry once said, "He whose head is in Heaven need not fear to put his feet in the grave!" Hallelujah! Our Father, who is in Heaven, we thank you!

Time to Reflect

- Are you sometimes overwhelmed by the battles you have to fight?
- Do you feel you are fighting alone?
- Have you prayed for an encounter with God that is new,

different, "outside the box" of you normality?

- Are you weary with the clouds that obscure your view of a good Father?

We worship a God who can see through the clouds and knows exactly what we need to draw us into more intimacy and closeness. If He has promised to protect, equip and shield us though the whole of our lives, whatever is thrown at us and however it makes us feel, can't we trust Him to lead us through those things into fresh revelations of His ultimate goodness and care?

God in Heaven is looking for an opportunity to tell you how much He loves you at this very moment. There is a Heaven full of conversation to be had between you and Him, Father to child. Some of it will be about you, some of it about Him. Some of it may be gentle discipline; some of it will be exuberant encouragement. Perhaps He wants to warn you, or teach you, or remind you of something. Sometimes He will sing over you a heavenly song, such as you have never heard before. Whatever God sends from Heaven, it will always be soaked in love and mercy and grace. Pray this prayer and wait expectantly for Him to come...

"I'm ready to see you Father; ready to hear You and ready to talk to You. There have been things that have clouded my view of Heaven; things that have got in the way and hidden the truth of who You are. I long to rise higher to feel the warmth of the sun. I don't always understand where you are in my life, but I know you see me all the time. I know your eyes are never off me and your ears are always attentive to my cry. There's lots I want to learn about You and about what heavenly rule is, because I know You have made me to enjoy it now while I'm alive, not just when I die. So please open Heaven above me, pour Your love over me, and let it spill out from me every place I go. Amen."

3. Above All Names

Provider ... Healer ... Shepherd ...

Let them praise the name of the Lord,
For His name alone is exalted;
His glory is above the earth and heaven.
Psalm 148:13

When someone calls out my name, I can't help but stop and listen. Why? Because my name is, to some extent, my identity. It's who I am. Even if there are five hundred other "Davids" in the room, I will still imagine the call has gone out to me.

The difference with God is there is only one of Him and His name is not just a title, it represents His character and His relationship to His people. God's name expresses His identity in multiple ways – Provider, Healer, Banner, Shepherd, Strong Tower, and so on.

The third phrase of The Lord's Prayer is, "Hallowed be your Name." The word "hallow" is an ancient one meaning "to make holy." You may have heard people talk about the hallowed halls of an academic establishment, which conjures up images of serious, studious types, reverently spending their days soaking up the contents of books in quiet libraries.

In Matthew's gospel, Jesus tells the disciples to hallow God's name when they address Him. In other words, to take His name seriously and treat it with reverence. When we pray this prayer, we are not just praying flippantly to a random person who might just prick up His ears in a room full of other gods. He is the holy God and by addressing Him by His "hallowed" name, we are placing Him in the highest possible place of honour and respect.

In the Old Testament, the Israelites were commanded to honour the hallowed name of God the Father and in return He would sanctify them as His people.

Therefore you shall keep My commandments, and perform them: I am the Lord. You shall not profane My holy name, but I will be hallowed among the children of Israel. I am the Lord who sanctifies you. Leviticus 22:31-32

In the New Testament, it is the name of Jesus, the Son of God, that opens up the way to salvation:

But as many as received Him, to them He gave the right to become children of God, to those who believe in His name. John 1:12

And it is to the name of Jesus that one day everyone will bow and confess Him as Lord (Philippians 2:10-11).

Isn't it wonderful that God's name contains such depth and mystery? Aren't you glad that He has a name that shows His character and can be applied to every single situation of our lives, no matter what we go through?

Our Father, in Heaven, hallowed is Your name!

Searching for truth

We live in a world where the name of God is used more often as a swear word than it is in prayer. People don't honour it, hallow it or respect it – which is incredibly sad.

But it doesn't mean that they have stopped searching for truth. I honestly believe that everyone has a God-shaped hole in their lives and they are looking to fill it with something meaningful. They may not pray using the name of the Almighty God of Israel, but it will be the name of another god, a philosophy, another person or, failing that, the latest luxury item on the market.

How do we stay true to the holy name of God in a world where so many alternatives are on offer to us? How do we help other people to encounter the Truth for themselves?

I want to look at a passage in Acts to see how Paul did it.

Paul in the lion's den!

Yes, I know it was Daniel who was thrown to the lions, but I like to think of this passage as the New Testament equivalent.

Paul and his friends had been travelling around Philippi, Corinth and Thessalonica ministering to people and seeing them saved, healed and delivered. Churches had sprung up in towns and cities as the Holy Spirit led both Gentiles and Jews into the truths contained in the gospel. In Acts chapter 16, Paul and Silas had been thrown in prison in Philippi for proclaiming Jesus, only to have a miraculous escape in front of a bewildered prison guard who promptly got saved along with his whole household. Amazing things were happening wherever Paul went.

By the next chapter, things changed. Paul is in Athens, the religious centre of Greece and a city given over to all sorts of godless mindsets and behaviours.

Now while Paul waited for them at Athens, his spirit was provoked within him when he saw that the city was given over to idols. Acts 17:16

The Athenians were so advanced in human knowledge and assumption that they were experts in free thinking. The atmosphere there provoked Paul's spirit and every day he reasoned with the Jews in the synagogue and the Gentiles in the market place, telling them about Jesus. Soon enough, the Epicurean and Stoic philosophers got to hear about what Paul was doing and they hauled him up to the Areopagus, a court on a hill, later called Mars Hill by the Romans, to defend his teaching. No longer was Paul standing on street corners preaching the gospel, he was bang in the middle of a crowd of intellectuals and sceptics who liked nothing better than to sit around all day debating the latest ideas.

For all the Athenians and the foreigners who were there spent their time in nothing else but either to tell or to hear some new thing. Acts 17:21

Who were the Epicureans?

Epicurus (341-270 BC) was a Greek philosopher who founded the school of Epicureanism, which taught that life was designed for happiness, not fear or pain, and whilst the philosophy didn't deny the existence of God, it taught that He was not involved in any way in the affairs of men. Logic was the ultimate strength of humanity and emotion was seen to be a weakness, so any pursuit of an emotional experience was not allowed. Any mistakes that humans made were made because in some way or another, emotions became too important. In some ways, we could see modern day humanism as coming from an Epicurean belief system.

A God-shaped hole

So here's Paul, a miracle-worker, in the middle of a court required to state his case for both the existence of God and His involvement in humanity through Jesus. Suddenly, he lands on an idea! He has seen the objects of worship in the Areopagus and noticed an altar bearing the inscription "To an unknown God". The Athenians were believers in the supernatural and by setting an altar to a god they didn't know, they were acknowledging there could be forces outside their understanding that had an influence on their world.

It was an altar to their God-shaped hole.

Even when Paul faces an attack on his faith by the protestations of humanists and intellectuals, he is able to stand before his accusers and focus on the altar to the god they have no name for.

Do you see?

Every man, woman and child who has ever existed, or will ever exist, is made to worship someone higher than they are. We are all made in God's image and we all have the heartbeat of a child needing to find its Father. In the face of a godless crowd, Paul begins to open up the truth of the God who is named and the God who is known.

"Our heart is restless until it rests in You," as St Augustine put it.

Preach it, Paul!

Let's look at how Paul brings the truth of God slap bang into the middle of deception.

You think you're not religious, but you are!

Do you know that it's often the case that people who claim to have no belief system at all are more religious than those who have. Paul makes an opening statement that is not one a preacher would necessarily make in the same way today.

He says, "*Men of Athens, I perceive that in all things you are very religious...*" (Acts 17:22).

He uses this statement provocatively to highlight the fact that despite all their intellect, and regardless of their professed atheism, they still live by a code of conduct that acknowledges there could be a god they don't yet know about. Paul takes the opportunity to introduce them to this God.

That's very clever!

You are worshipping Him without knowing!

You know, the devil can't keep us away from the reality of God, he can only deflect us from the reality. The nearest many people get to the Creator is through creation and God will speak through His creation every second of every day. We are created beings. We have a body, a soul and a spirit and God has designed us in such a way that we will never be fully at rest or in peace until we are attached in worship to our Creator.

To worship creation, or a system of belief such as humanism or atheism, is to deny the truth that God, the name above every other name, is the Being behind it all and the Sustainer of it all.

Paul tells the Athenians that they are worshipping something – but they don't know what. It has no name, no personality and they can't interact with it, but he knows the God who made the world and everything in it. I wonder what they thought at this moment?

God, who made the world and everything in it, since He is Lord of heaven and earth, does not dwell in temples made with hands. Nor is He worshipped with men's hands, as though He needed anything, since He gives to all life, breath, and all things. And He has made from one blood every nation of men to dwell on all the face of the earth, and has determined their pre-appointed times and the boundaries of their dwellings, so that they should seek the Lord, in the hope that they might grope for Him and find Him, though He is not far from each one of us; for in Him we live and move and have our being, as also some of your own poets have said, 'For we are also His offspring.' Therefore, since we are the offspring of God, we ought not to think that the Divine Nature is like gold or silver or stone, something shaped by art and man's devising. Acts 17: 24-29

If we understand, then, that there are a lot of people out there who, in their own way, want to worship God but haven't found Him yet, why won't we be more compassionate towards them?

If people didn't want to know God, why would they pray when someone in their family is sick? Why do they have their children christened? They may not understand all of it, but they don't want their kids to go to hell when they die.

Don't mock people who are searching for God but don't know it. Such were some of you! Paul doesn't mock the Epicureans and he is not aggressive or judgemental towards them. He wants them to meet the hallowed God who they are endeavouring to worship in the wrong way, maybe, but with no less sincerity.

People outside the Christian faith can say truth but they don't know truth. We will never win people for Jesus if we don't understand that they can say what is true without being Christians.

I am amazed sometimes at how people of other faiths can lead better lives than some Christians. The devotion of a Sikh who wears a turban puts to shame the Christian who won't wear a cross. The reverence that a Muslim has for the Koran is a challenge to the Christian who never opens his Bible.

We worship God who is, "the Way the Truth and the Life" (John 14:6). We should be ready to take time with those who also worship Him but don't yet know it, as Paul did.

Truly, these times of ignorance God overlooked, but now commands all men everywhere to repent, because He has appointed a day on which He will judge the world in righteousness by the Man whom He has ordained. He has given assurance of this to all by raising Him from the dead. Acts 17:30-31

Paul says, "I know who He is!" He doesn't just leave them with information but offers them an invitation.

There is something they need to do in order to get to know God: repent. In response, some of those present sneered and mocked him, but the end of this chapter tells us that others who had listened to the message of salvation believed it and proceeded to join with Paul.

What Paul basically said was, "I know the I AM." I think this is one of the most incredible names of God because it's open-ended. It's not "I WAS" and it's not "I WILL BE" but it rests in the present tense eternally. God is always "I AM" and because of it, the past, present and future are all linked into the NOW! Whatever we face, He is "I AM!"

Hallelujah!

God's beautiful names

Every time I think I have come to the end of the meaning of God's name, I find another one. There is no limit to His love and power, and each of His names speaks of an aspect of His nature and character that draws me closer to Him. If God had limited names there would be certain things He couldn't do and, as we know, God can't be contained by anyone or anything.

In Islam, there are ninety-nine names for God and not one of them means "love". I don't want to offend anyone by writing this, but it does help us understand why there is a lot of frustration in the faith, as there is no security there that comes through being unconditionally loved. I can't possibly list all the names of God here because it would take too long. But here are a few to be going on with!

He's the bread (John 6:35). He feeds us with everything that nourishes our soul.

He's the Good Shepherd (John 10:11). He takes care of us and protects us when we are under threat from the enemy.

He's the Door (John 10:9). He welcomes us and leads us into safety. With Jesus there is always a way in and always a way out.

I remember once how I arrived at church and locked my keys in the boot of my car. Someone kindly took me all the way home where, miraculously, I found the spare set of keys and was able to open up the car and retrieve the other set. That day I knew the value of an open door!

He's the Rose of Sharon (Song of Solomon 2:1). He is fragrant and sweet. Do you get upset when you run out of perfume or aftershave? God will never lose His fragrance. He is the aroma of your praise. Not only that, He loves your fragrance too!

Our God is the Lord who heals, He is the Alpha and the Omega, He is the blood of the new Covenant, the Resurrection and the Life. He comforts, has mercy, makes all things, sustains all things, is our Saviour, friend and deliverer. He is with us always and His name is holy.

Are you glad you have a God like that?

Let this mind be in you which was also in Christ Jesus, who, being in the form of God, did not consider it robbery to be equal with God, but made Himself of no reputation, taking the form of a bondservant, and coming in the likeness of men. And being found in appearance as a man, He humbled Himself and became obedient to the point of death, even the death of the cross. Therefore God also has highly exalted Him and given Him the name which is above every name, that at the name of Jesus every knee should bow, of those in heaven, and of those on earth, and of those under the earth, and that every tongue should confess that Jesus Christ is Lord, to the glory of God the Father. Philippians 2:5-11

Time to Reflect

- What are the names of God that mean the most to you?
- Do you have stories of the times He has shown His love through the meaning of those names?
- Would you know what to say to someone genuinely searching for God?

Meditate

God wants all men, women and children to encounter His love. His holiness doesn't mean He wants to stay away from anything impure or dirty. He is not a King in an ivory tower, He is a Father who sent His Son into an unclean world to make it clean again. Take time now to think about the names of God that make this a reality for you today. You may need a shepherd to lead you, a warrior to fight for you, a light to guide you or a physician to heal you. There is nothing you will face that God cannot deal with and lead you through. Let's thank Him for it.

"Father, Your name is holy. I am all too often aware how much I fall short from holiness and I want to tell you today how glad I am that you still accept me. I know You love me, and I know you understand me. Father, when I think about all Your names, I am deeply grateful that every one of them reflects the truth of who You are and what You are like. There is no other God like You! I'd like to share You with others in ways they can understand and

I'm asking You to help me to do that without being judgemental, derisive or defensive. You want everyone to meet You and I want to be someone who helps make that possible. For the sake of the One who gave everything for the world You made. Amen."

4. The Approaching Kingdom

Your kingdom is an everlasting kingdom,
And Your dominion endures throughout all generations.
Psalm 145:13

What is a kingdom? The Oxford English Dictionary describes it as "a country, state or territory ruled by a king or queen". Put another way, a king or queen can't actually fulfil their role unless they have a kingdom over which they rule and reign. All the trappings of the monarchy would be worthless and seem rather ridiculous if there was no kingdom over which they could preside.

The same is true for God, but His rule is different. The verse above says, His Kingdom is an everlasting kingdom, which means that it is not restricted to the laws and governance of any human monarch. In fact, it is from God that all our nation's kings and queens throughout history have been given their right to rule.

A different kind of King

For centuries before Jesus, the Israelites had been looking for a physical king to build a physical kingdom that would release them from captivity and oppression and establish them as a major world power. In the Old Testament, God had manifested Himself through practical ways in order to liberate His people both physically and spiritually. More than that, the Old Testament is rich with stories of God using the tangible to reveal the invisible. When Moses stands shoeless in front of the burning bush, even though he doesn't realise it until the end, he has just encountered the presence of God in tangible form, which we call a theophany. God is revealing Himself in visible ways from His place of invisibility.

So when the Lord saw that he turned aside to look, God called to him from the midst of the bush and said, 'Moses, Moses!' And he said, 'Here I am.' Then He said, 'Do not draw near this place. Take your sandals off your feet, for the place where you stand is holy ground.' Moreover He said, 'I am the God of your father—the God of Abraham, the God of Isaac, and the God of Jacob.' And Moses hid his face, for he was afraid to look upon God. Exodus 3:4-6

When He came to live among us, Jesus took this further by revealing how God's invisible Kingdom is freely accessible and available to each and every person, man woman and child, to heal bodies, minds and spirits without reserve.

He came as a King, but not in the way the Israelites expected. They wanted a warrior on a horse, but He came humbly on a donkey. They wanted a King who would destroy, but He repaired. They cried out for a King who would condemn, but He came to forgive.

His kingdom is not of this world!

Throughout His earthly ministry, Jesus often spoke about the

Kingdom of God, regularly using parables to illustrate His point, as we shall see later. For Jesus, the manifestation of the Kingdom was central to all He was, and to all God is. It was for "now", marked by the in-breaking of the miraculous, and for the future when God's rule will be fully established once and for all.

Jesus taught on how to enter the Kingdom:

For I say to you, that unless your righteousness exceeds the righteousness of the scribes and Pharisees, you will by no means enter the kingdom of heaven. Matthew 5:20

And how, when He comes again, His Kingdom will be established;

When the Son of Man comes in His glory, and all the holy angels with Him, then He will sit on the throne of His glory. All the nations will be gathered before Him, and He will separate them one from another, as a shepherd divides his sheep from the goats. And He will set the sheep on His right hand, but the goats on the left. Then the King will say to those on His right hand, 'Come, you blessed of My Father, inherit the kingdom prepared for you from the foundation of the world.' Matthew 25:31-34

A different kind of Kingdom

Jesus answered, 'My kingdom is not of this world.' John 18:36

The boast of the British Empire was that the sun never went down on its kingdom, as it was so vast that there was always daylight somewhere. The Roman Empire covered the whole of Europe as we know it today. The Greeks influenced millions with their philosophies and the Egyptians gave us mathematics, design and architecture. But the empires, kingdoms and rulers of this world eventually pass away, leaving legacies of both glory and catastrophe behind them.

God's Kingdom is unique. It will never pass away. He is King of Heaven and King of all He has created. You say, "That's obvious, of course He is!" But how often do we forget it? How easy it is to view God as a remote, benign old man who sits in Heaven watching us from afar while we get on with our own lives. How often we forget that we have full access to the rights and privileges of the King.

He is not a Prince of some principality like Monte Carlo. He doesn't potter around making occasional public appearances to his subjects. No! The Bible tells us He is ever present and always available to us, His children.

God is our refuge and strength,

a very present help in trouble.

Therefore we will not fear,

Even though the earth be removed,

And though the mountains be carried into the midst of the sea;

Though its waters roar and be troubled,

Though the mountains shake with its swelling.

There is a river whose streams shall make glad the city of God,

The holy place of the tabernacle of the Most High.

God is in the midst of her, she shall not be moved;

God shall help her, just at the break of dawn.

The nations raged, the kingdoms were moved;

He uttered His voice, the earth melted.

The Lord of hosts is with us;

The God of Jacob is our refuge. Psalm 46:1-7

He has no one above Him and His rule is high above any other. It is unique and encompasses everything, everywhere. Yes, His presence is in Heaven where He is seated, but it is also in His world He has made. So when we pray, Your Kingdom come we are asking for more of Heaven's rule to come into our earthly experience. It's freely available all the time.

Well, hallelujah for that!

If we fully understand this, it will transform our perception of who God is and what His authority and rule is like. It will also help us to understand that those other than Him are lesser in status. The Christian message is about the King of Kings and the Lord of Lords. He may battle with the principalities and powers and the prince of the air on our behalf, but He has never lost and will never lose His place as King of His Kingdom.

I hope you are getting it!

So how does God's Kingdom manifest itself on earth?

His Kingdom is about belonging

How do we get into any kingdom or country? Well, there are rules aren't there? We need to carry a passport from our own country in order to be ready to display it to any official who asks to see it.

I am a citizen of the United Kingdom and the first page of my passport reads,

"Her Britannic Majesty's Secretary of State requests and requires in the name of Her Majesty all those whom it may concern to allow the bearer to pass freely without let or hindrance, and to afford the bearer such assistance and protection as may be necessary."

Our passports allow us to travel under the protection of the Queen as citizens of her realm.

As a child of the King of Kings I could substitute any title of God into the above statement, because I don't just belong to an earthly kingdom of her Majesty, I belong to a Heavenly Kingdom of my Father. In Him I have free access to boldly approach His throne through the veil and onto His lap. As I belong to Him, I also can pass freely anywhere I like, because no weapon formed against me will prosper. That is my right! It's not a privilege reserved for the few, it's my right as a child of God! I belong to Him and come under His rule and protection because He loves me.

How exciting is that? If the truth of this could only sink in to each and every one of us, we would not be sitting in bondage any more. We are free because Jesus made it possible on the cross and we belong in His Kingdom.

Stand fast therefore in the liberty by which Christ has made us free, and do not be entangled again with a yoke of bondage. Galatians 5:1

His Kingdom is about repentance

Having said all that, let's not forget that we enter the Kingdom of God through the door of repentance. His door is always open, but we have to choose to walk through it. Unlike when we are born in an earthly sense and we inherit our parents' nationality, in a spiritual sense we have to choose to be born again by accepting Jesus as Lord of our lives.

Let me illustrate my point.

As a society, we have tried multiculturalism and although some of it has worked, some of it hasn't. Sometimes people from other cultures and traditions prefer not to adopt aspects of a country as their own. They remain visitors in a foreign land as they choose to live alongside each other, but decide not to integrate by keeping their own language, religion and friendships very much tied into their own traditions. In Australia they have tried to do it differently. Anyone can visit, but if they want to become an Australian national, they are required to salute the country's flag, engage in the culture and adapt as well as adopt. It's not just about saying, "G'day" and hoping for the best!

In the same way, if we want to belong to the Kingdom of God, we have to adopt and adapt. It is not good enough just to talk the talk, we have to walk the walk, and that requires repentance. I'm not saying for one minute that we all have to be the same, look the same and act the same – that would be awful! But we do have to have one thing in common in that we have decided to follow the King and live as children of His Kingdom with all its freedoms and all its boundaries.

When I'm called to help pastors who have gone astray I ask the leaders or other people in their church, "How did you find out he'd done wrong?" They say, "What do you mean?" I reply, "Well, did he turn himself in or did you catch him?" If they tell me the pastor was caught in the act or found out some other way, I will respond, "Then the tears are very likely because of the grief of being found out rather than genuine tears of repentance, so you are going to find it difficult to restore him."

True repentance is much more than just saying sorry. When King David was sinning through his back teeth and Nathan the prophet told him a story to open up David's heart to his own sin, David eventually got it and replied,

I have sinned against the Lord. 2 Samuel 12:13

Following the revelation of his own wrongdoing, he came to God with a broken and repentant spirit and wrote Psalm 51, which drips with David's sorrow and his desperation for forgiveness and reconnection to God.

Repentance literally means to think again or to change one's mind. It is not about saying sorry, it is about turning around to do things differently. It is about accepting our need of God and how, if we are to live as children of the King, we can invite Him to change our heart, which leads to a change in our behaviour. It's like we are reborn.

So I guess you could say: no repentance, no entrance! Read how Jesus describes it to Nicodemus in the Gospel of John:

Jesus answered and said to him, 'Most assuredly, I say to you, unless one is born again, he cannot see the kingdom of God.'

Nicodemus said to Him, 'How can a man be born when he is old? Can he enter a second time into his mother's womb and be born? Jesus answered, 'Most assuredly, I say to you, unless one is born of water and the Spirit, he cannot enter the kingdom of God. That which is born of the flesh is flesh, and that which is born of the Spirit is spirit. Do not marvel that I said to you, 'You must be born again.' The wind blows where it wishes, and you hear the sound of it, but cannot tell where it comes from and where it goes. So is everyone who is born of the Spirit.' (John 3:3-8)

His Kingdom is about healing

Then Jesus went about all the cities and villages, teaching in their synagogues, preaching the gospel of the kingdom, and healing every sickness and every disease among the people. Matthew 9:35

When we pray, "Your kingdom come", we should expect that which comes in response to be filled with the same power which flowed through Jesus during His earthly ministry. Jesus told His disciples that they would do greater things than He did when the Holy Spirit came upon them (John 14:12) and the same is true for us today.

When God's Kingdom comes, healing will follow. It is not a powerless, limp Kingdom – it is one full of grace and mercy, compassion and love. The Bible tells us that it was when Jesus was moved with compassion that He healed the sick and the more He did, the freer people became and the more His fame spread.

Healing is a criterion of the Kingdom. That's the bottom line.

His Kingdom is about provision

We live in a rights-based society which encourages people to take legal action against one another for easy financial gain. If there's a quick buck to be had, we take it by right, without considering the deeper cost to our inner state of mind. We may get a boost to our bank balance, but we could also have compromised our integrity along the way.

Greed is not part of God's Kingdom. In fact, Jesus would often speak out strongly against it in parables and to people He encountered along the way, who were bound up by it like the rich young ruler in Luke 18:18-23.

For us, His children, God is able to provide for our every need because He is our Father, our Daddy. All He requires of us in return is to focus our attention not on the anxieties about our money situation or where we should live, or even the debt we may be in, but on Him and on His Kingdom.

Jesus spoke directly into those fears at the Sermon on the Mount.

But seek first the kingdom of God and His righteousness, and all these things shall be added to you. (Matthew 6:33

Did you need to hear this today? Have you become overwhelmed by anxiety and fear? Take a minute to hand everything over to God again and thank Him that He is your Provider and recommit to seeking Him first, before anything else.

It just gets things in the right order doesn't it?

His Kingdom is about strategy

Do we belong to a Kingdom that doesn't know where it's going? Is it aimless and vague with a wishy-washy message? Absolutely not! Jesus modelled the most amazing strategy for us by telling us to forgive as He forgave, lay our lives down as He laid His life down, heal the sick as He healed the sick and pray to our Father as He prayed to His Father. Like Him, we are to love the un-loveable, kiss the un-kissable and welcome the un-welcomeable. He invites us to do whatever He did when He was on earth and be led by the

Holy Spirit to do what He is doing today. Even though the Kingdom of God is unseen, we can still see the results of it.

God knows what He wants for His world and He knows how to achieve it. He could do it all Himself, sweeping across the planet making everything perfect, but then there would be no room for us to choose to follow Him. A huge part of His strategy is to partner with us in furthering His Kingdom on Earth. That's one of the reasons the Holy Spirit came! Don't waste the opportunities God gives you. He trusts you with His strategy because you are part of His Kingdom army and part of His Kingdom family.

And Jesus, walking by the Sea of Galilee, saw two brothers, Simon called Peter, and Andrew his brother, casting a net into the sea; for they were fishermen. Then He said to them, 'Follow Me, and I will make you fishers of men.' They immediately left their nets and followed Him. Matthew 4:18-20

"I want to tell you a story"

On many different occasions, Jesus used parables to describe what the Kingdom of God was like to help people understand it better.

The parables, if we could understand them fully would totally transform our theology. Far from being simple and twee fairy tales, they are rich with meaning and have layers of truth that continue to surprise us no matter how long we have been Christians. Don't give up reading them because you think you know them. The chances are a new nugget of revelation will drop into your spirit and God will speak to you afresh.

The parables of the Kingdom in Matthew 13 contain deep-seated theological issues broken down into understandable stories to help us understand both the culture of the day and the relevance in Jesus' teaching for today. In these two verses below Jesus explains to His disciples that the crowd needed to hear stories because they had not received the same revelation of truth that the disciples had been given.

And the disciples came and said to Him, 'Why do You speak to them in parables?' He answered and said to them, 'Because it has been given to you to know the mysteries of the Kingdom of Heaven, but to them it has not been given.' Matthew 13:10-11

The Parable of the Sower, which comes before, is all about the Kingdom of God. Jesus warns about the different reactions people can have to the message of salvation, whether it is those who allow the enemy to snatch the truth away from them straight away, or those who start off well only to reject God when times get tough. Ignorance and hardness of heart is behind the illustration. Jesus is not talking about backsliding, He is talking about those who refuse to hear and understand the beauty of the gospel; those who, when God comes to them, deaf it out and ignore it. Jesus says these people are not in the Kingdom!

It's a sobering story, so don't expect me to be nice about it. I want to write and preach about it boldly because that's how Jesus did it. I have read the words of Jesus over two solid years and it's because of that I can write with integrity and conviction.

Jesus is deadly serious about the dangers of compromise. Just because you are in church and have nice Christian friends it doesn't mean you actually belong to it. Your walk with God is your walk with God – you are responsible for it and the way you live your life, as am I. Just because you have prayed the prayer and entered the Kingdom of God doesn't mean you belong in it. It takes discipline and humility and obedience and commitment, but my word, the rewards are plentiful!

I want to be known by my fruit, don't you? I don't want to be the seed that withered and died or got taken away by the birds. I want to root myself in this Kingdom so that when I pray "Your

Kingdom come" I mean it with every ounce of my being, because it actually means something to me and isn't just something I say out of boring routine from a pew on a Sunday morning.

The remaining parables in Matthew chapter 13 continue the theme of the Kingdom. The Parable of the Wheat and the Tares, for example, explains how, because wheat and tares look so similar it is easy to think they are the same. But the farmer knows the difference. Jesus is warning the people how easy it is to look like you are spiritual, but in reality there is no spiritual fruit coming through because you are faking it.

What is the fruit of the Spirit? Let's remind ourselves.

But the fruit of the Spirit is love, joy, peace, longsuffering, kindness, goodness, faithfulness, gentleness, self-control. Against such there is no law. Galatians 5:22-23

We have a King whose Kingdom is built on these characteristics because this is who He is! We live in the days of the Kingdom of God and if that doesn't excite you I don't know what will! I am passionate about honouring my King, just as I honour the Queen of my country who God has given us to rule over our land.

So pray with me,

Father, let Your Kingdom come!

Time to Reflect

Mother Teresa once said,

"Let us more and more insist on raising funds of love, of kindness, of understanding, of peace. Money will come if we seek first the Kingdom of God – the rest will be given."

She never once failed to pay a bill and she fed up to 9,000 people every day. This is Kingdom language!

- Read Matthew chapter 13
- Is God revealing new truths to you about His Kingdom?
- Are you committed to hearing His word and obeying it?
- What evidences of the Kingdom of God are around you?
- What are you hungry to see more of?

Meditate

The Kingdom of God is here and it is now. When you received the Holy Spirit, you were filled with the same power that raised Jesus from the dead who enables you to do even more than Jesus did when He was on earth. It's like you are a walking piece of Heaven! In Jesus, nothing is impossible: no sickness un-healable, no depression un-liftable, no situation unresolvable. Being a child of the King gives you the right to behave like one, so enjoy the gifts and fruits He gives you. He's your Father and He wants you to be free to relish the opportunities to bring Heaven to Earth. If you are ready for more of the wonderful Holy Spirit in your life (and to be honest, why wouldn't you be?!) then pray with me:

"Holy Spirit, I honour you as my friend. You are the presence of God who lives in me and You bring me life, peace, joy and comfort. You also convict me of my wrongdoing without condemning me and You lead me into freedom when I choose to be forgiven and learn to forgive myself. I love to imagine what we could do together to spread the beauty of Your Kingdom to a world that is so thirsty for it. Please come and fill me because I can't do it without You – and I don't want to try doing it without You, either. Lead me into all truth and let me see more and more of the miracles I know are the expression of Your love, Father, to the world You made and Jesus, to the world you died to save. Thank you. Amen."

5. Obedience

Your will be done

Jesus answered and said to him, 'If anyone loves Me, he will keep My word; and My Father will love him, and We will come to him and make Our home with him. He who does not love Me does not keep My words; and the word which you hear is not Mine but the Father's who sent Me.'

John 14:23-24

What does it really mean to obey someone? One definition of obedience is that it is "compliance with an order, request, or law or submission to another's authority" (Oxford English Dictionary).

Is this what it means to obey God?

When Jesus taught the disciples to pray, "Your will be done..." did that mean they had to just submit to a bunch of rules and orders barked out from God in Heaven, who wanted everything done His way and His way alone? What does it mean for us today? What is God's will for us and how do we find it?

Who do I obey?

It's fashionable these days for a bride to omit the word "obey" from the vows made to her husband-to-be, choosing instead to "cherish" or "honour". There's nothing wrong with that on one level, but it does imply that we have lost something as a society if we are uncomfortable with the concept of obedience.

News reports are packed full of stories of rebellious teenagers running riot, unruly children in schools overpowering their teachers, and adults who flaunt the laws of the land and think nothing of beating up or abusing the policemen sent to establish order and authority.

Society needs boundaries and people need to know who is in charge. Whether they like it or not, people need someone to obey. People need to be able to trust their authority figures and not be controlled by them. When God organised the nation of Israel, He passed on His Law to Moses not to repress the people but to give them security. To obey the Ten Commandments would result in a society that ran smoothly and whose people respected one another under God.

And Moses went up to God, and the Lord called to him from the mountain, saying, 'Thus you shall say to the house of Jacob, and tell the children of Israel: "You have seen what I did to the Egyptians, and how I bore you on eagles' wings and brought you to Myself. Now therefore, if you will indeed obey My voice and keep My covenant, then you shall be a special treasure to Me above all people; for all the earth is Mine. And you shall be to Me a kingdom of priests and a holy nation." These are the words which you shall speak to the children of Israel.' Exodus 19:3-6

Aren't you relieved that in the United Kingdom we have laws that keep us from complete anarchy and mob rule? I am! The current oath of allegiance sworn by many in the role of public service, such as the police, parliamentarians, judges and magistrates, includes the promise to be faithful and bear true allegiance to the monarch with God's help. In other words, these servants of the land have promised that for as long as they hold office, they will be obedient to those in ultimate authority – God and, in our time, Queen Elizabeth the Second.

Year by year it seems like our nation is becoming increasingly secular and most of us will have witnessed disorder of some kind, either first hand or in the media. But praise God we are still built on strong foundations! That's something to be grateful for and we need to keep praying for the Queen and her Government to rule with justice and mercy in the years to come.

What breaks God's heart?

The book of Isaiah opens with a sad story of how God's heart has been broken by the unfaithfulness of the Israelite nation. They had become wayward and rebellious and their identity as God's special people had become polluted by strangers. God mourns the loss of His relationship with His people:

I have nourished and brought up children,
And they have rebelled against Me;
The ox knows its owner
And the donkey its master's crib;
But Israel does not know,
My people do not consider. Isaiah 1:2b-4

The prophet Isaiah continues,
Alas, sinful nation,
A people laden with iniquity,
A brood of evildoers,
Children who are corrupters!

They have forsaken the Lord,

They have provoked to anger

The Holy One of Israel,

They have turned away backward. Isaiah 1:4

God talks to the children of Israel expressing His sadness that after all He has done in nourishing and loving them, they have turned their backs on Him, using the blessings He has poured out on them to become corrupt. They have provoked Him to anger and He tells them they are in a mess, sick with wrong thinking and wrongdoing.

God has had enough of their apologies, their sacrifices and their burnt offerings. He is fed up to the back teeth with the blood of lambs and the smells of incense. He would rather they stop saying sorry all the time, because they only carry on doing the same things once they have paid lip service with a sacrifice or two.

I cannot endure iniquity and the sacred meeting.

Your New Moons and your appointed feasts

My soul hates;

They are a trouble to Me,

I am weary of bearing them.

When you spread out your hands,

I will hide My eyes from you;

Even though you make many prayers,

I will not hear.

Your hands are full of blood. Isaiah 1:13b-15

What God really wants is that they change their ways and return to Him.

When I was on holiday one year, I saw a man beat up his wife and the following day I saw him again by the pool with her, only this time he was pleading for her forgiveness. I could see that he thought saying sorry to her would make everything better, but to be honest, I'm not sure it did, and actually, I don't think the word, "sorry" is ever good enough on it's own. Everyone makes mistakes, but we have to learn from them and change our behaviour. A bit like this man by the pool, the Israelites thought that God could be bought with a sacrifice of penitent behaviour so that He was happy, leaving them free to live their lives however they wanted.

In the end, as far as God is concerned, obedience is so much better than sacrifice. Read what the Bible says:

So Samuel said 'Has the Lord as great delight in burnt offerings and sacrifices, as in obeying the voice of the Lord? Behold, to obey is better than sacrifice, and to heed than the fat of rams.' 1 Samuel 15:22

What makes God angry?

Never think you can do God a favour or patronise Him with your acts of service. Notice the verse that follows the one above in 1 Samuel 15:

For rebellion is as the sin of witchcraft, and stubbornness is as iniquity and idolatry. Because you have rejected the word of the Lord He also has rejected you from being king. 1 Samuel 15:23

How easily we think that if we have worked hard in church, gone on a mission trip or two to help the poor, or given time and money to a worthy cause, we have made God so happy that He will ignore our dabbling in immoral behaviours or our preoccupation with the "gods" that feed our selfish desires. We can become so puffed up with our own virtue that we forget how much God hates our rebellion and hates our pride.

There are no brownie points in Heaven for good behaviour because God has no desire for burnt offerings and acts of service that cover up our rebellious ways. To Him, they are the same as the sin of witchcraft and He wants nothing to do with them. Not only that, but when people's hearts are hard and stubborn, God takes it very seriously indeed, likening it to sin and the selfishness that comes from setting yourself and your opinions above God. When He is rejected in this way, it makes God very angry, as it is a deliberate attack on His will and His goodness.

Obedience God's way

Sometimes I think that some Christians believe obedience to be a lot harder than it actually is. They go around believing that the Christian life is tight with conditions on how to live, speak, think, dress and so on, and that the Bible is just a set of rules. I can tell you that if that's what is was I wouldn't be interested in it!

Obedience God's way must come from the heart of a person. The value is not in the things we achieve but in what motivates us to do them in the first place.

Let me explain.

My wife, Molly and I have, in the past, been unfortunate enough to be the victims of a robbery. If you have been through it, you will know that it is a difficult thing to come to terms with. For us it was not so much about the loss of electrical items or other such household stuff, but because the most precious items that were taken had a value far beyond the pounds and pence.

Molly had a ring taken from her that was her Mum's wedding ring. On the surface it was "just" a ring, but the deep loss that Molly felt was due to the emotional significance it carried. In fact, I will go so far as to say that we would rather have given the person who took it it's full monetary value rather than see it disappear forever. Molly's Mum's ring can never be replaced. When we lost the engagement ring I had made for her, the insurance enabled us to buy another one.

But Molly told me it would never be her actual engagement ring – it wasn't the same one I gave her when she was twenty-five.

Similarly, the true value of following Jesus is not in the outward appearance or outward acts, it is in the heart. Our faith has its foundation in a relationship between child and Father and is made possible by the death and resurrection of Jesus. So it follows then, that whilst there are some times when obedience to God is difficult, there will be other times when it is easy! That's the nature of a love relationship. Sometimes, there is no sacrifice in our obedience because it is simply an act of putting our hand into His loving hand as a child does to their parent.

For a person to willingly submit to the will of another, there has to be a number of contrasting ingredients. The act of obedience or submission to God's will is manifested in both our freedom to choose our own way as well as our surrender to His perfect will.

What does that mean? How do we submit to God's will for our lives but also keep our own free will to choose the way we want to live?

How Paul saw it

I know this is a long passage from Scripture here, but it's so great I didn't want to miss any of it out! Read with me what Paul says about the spread of sin throughout the whole world and how, through the act of obedience of one man to the will of His Father, its power over us was destroyed once and for all.

Therefore, just as through one man sin entered the world, and death through sin, and thus death spread to all men, because all sinned (for until the law sin was in the world, but sin is not imputed when there is no law. Nevertheless death reigned from Adam to Moses, even over those who had not sinned according to the likeness of the transgression of Adam, who is a type of Him who was to come. But the free gift is not like the offense. For if by the one man's offense many died, much more the grace of God and the gift by the grace of the one Man, Jesus Christ, abounded to many. And the gift is not like that which came through the one who sinned. For the judgment which came from one offense, resulted in condemnation, but the free gift which came from many offenses resulted in justification. For if by the one man's offense death reigned through the one, much more those who receive abundance of grace and of the gift of righteousness will reign in life through the One, Jesus Christ). Therefore, as through one man's offense judgment came to all men, resulting in condemnation, even so through one Man's righteous act the free gift came to all men, resulting in justification of life. For as by one man's disobedience many were made sinners, so also by one Man's obedience many will be made righteous. Romans 5:12-19

When Jesus suggested we pray "Your will be done," He was really saying, "Lord, rather than me choose to do what I will do, I will choose what You would want me to do. So Lord, I do not negate my choice, I make my choice Your choice!"

We never lose our choice when we surrender in obedience to our Father in Heaven. If we did, there would be no love.

Is someone who is totally surrendered to the will of God a zombie? Absolutely not! They become a warrior in whom sin has no dominion and power to be a slave any longer. When we are obedient to the One who has freed us we become righteous and we don't feel condemned or restricted any longer. Now that's exciting! I am not a slave to Christ through oppression, but a slave by choice to the freedom offered by the work of the Cross!

Hallelujah!

What then? Shall we sin because we are not under law but under grace? Certainly not! Do you not know that to whom you present yourselves slaves to obey, you are that one's slave whom you obey, whether of sin leading to death, or of obedience leading to righteousness? But God be thanked that though you were slaves of sin, yet you obeyed from the heart that form of doctrine to which you were delivered. Romans 6:15-17

By saying "Your will be done," we don't become clones, we become more and more Christlike, having the power of God within us by the power of the Holy Spirit to defeat sin in our human nature.

It's time to get excited about this!

It's mind-blowing, it's fantastic and it is the best and the greatest of everything there ever has been or ever will be. As I obey my Father and submit to Him, I become more and more free to live my life as He made it to be lived, growing in righteousness and the knowledge of God.

Aren't you grateful?

So tell Him right now.

"Father, sometimes I have to just stop everything and think about the enormity of what you have given me. You gave Your Son Jesus to open wide the door before me into a life jam-packed with heavenly blessings and I am deeply thankful for it as well as being constantly amazed that You love me that much. Please keep encouraging me to walk into more of You."

I want end this chapter by looking into the life of the greatest man that has ever or will ever walk this earth. As fully human and fully divine, Jesus is our inspiration, our encouragement, our hope, our helpmeet and our friend. There is no one else to whom we can or should look as the perfect example of a life fully submitted to the will of the Father.

When Jesus submitted

Obviously it wasn't just in the Garden of Gethsemane that Jesus submitted to His Heavenly Father, but this is the clearest example of the rawness of surrender and the glory that followed it.

Then Jesus came with them to a place called Gethsemane, and said to the disciples, 'Sit here while I go and pray over there.' And He took with Him Peter and the two sons of Zebedee, and He began to be sorrowful and deeply distressed. Then He said to them, 'My soul is exceedingly sorrowful, even to death. Stay here and watch with Me.' Matthew 26:36-38

Jesus was nearing the end of His life. Events had taken a rapid turn for the worse and He knew what was likely to be ahead and it was not going to be pleasant. Here, His soul is full of sorrow and distress. He is anxious and tense and His nerves are on edge. He would have known all about crucifixion as a method of execution – that it was the most horrific death known to the human race.

Whenever a Roman citizen was sentenced to execution for a crime, he was invariably beheaded, since crucifixion was considered too brutal for anyone but an enemy of Rome. This is what Jesus was to face and in Gethsemane, aged only 33. He began to pray to His Father.

How Jesus submitted

And He was withdrawn from them about a stone's throw, and He knelt down and prayed, saying, 'Father, if it is Your will, take this cup away from Me; nevertheless not My will, but Yours, be done.' Then an angel appeared to Him from heaven, strengthening Him. And being in agony, He prayed more earnestly. Then His sweat became like great drops of blood falling down to the ground. Luke 22:41-44

Jesus never asks us to do what He has not already done. His willingness to become sin for us took Him right to the edge of His own humanity. At any point He could have clicked into His divinity and shaken off the requirement to go through with the cross, but He didn't. The trauma caused Him to sweat drops of blood – a medical condition which only occurs under extreme stress when the blood vessels rupture and the blood infiltrates the sweat glands. Jesus' body was subject to the same limitations as every other Christian, but without the sinful consequences. He felt hunger, thirst, pain, weariness and exhaustion.

Here, Jesus has fully submitted Himself to His Father. He is willing to have no authority unless His Father wills it. He knew that if His Father didn't raise Him from the dead He would be gone forever. Jesus hurled Himself into the power of the Father and the Holy Spirit and became as vulnerable as you and I can be, so we can be as confident as He is now.

I can of Myself do nothing. As I hear, I judge; and My judgment is righteous, because I do not seek My own will but the will of the Father who sent Me. John 5:30

Why Jesus submitted

For He made Him who knew no sin to be sin for us, that we might become the righteousness of God in Him. 2 Corinthians 5:21

Jesus submitted to the will of His Father in order that we might be made righteous. Because He did this, all authority was given to Him and there is no other name given to man whereby we can be saved (Acts 4:12).

Jesus gave up the right to live in His own will to also demonstrate what ultimate obedience to the Father is like. We will, because of His sacrifice, never be required to do what He has done because His death broke the power of the enemy once and for all. Paul says that anyone who wishes to experience a deeper knowledge of Christ needs to be willing to enter into His suffering and death.

What a comfort it is to know that we have a God who has gone before us in everything? Jesus obedience to death on a cross can never be out-sacrificed. He has done it all and every time we face a decision for or against submission to the Father's best will for us, we can remember what Jesus has accomplished.

What a God! What a Saviour!

Let this mind be in you which was also in Christ Jesus, who, being in the form of God, did not consider it robbery to be equal with God, but made Himself of no reputation, taking the form of a bondservant, and coming in the likeness of men. And being found in appearance as a man, He humbled Himself and became obedient to the point of death, even the death of the cross. Therefore God also has highly exalted Him and given Him the name which is above every name, that at the name of Jesus every knee should bow, of those in heaven, and of those on earth, and of those under the earth, and that every tongue should confess that Jesus Christ is Lord, to the glory of God the Father. Philippians 2:5-11

Can I submit?

Now if Jesus did all that and submitted to His own Father, what is going to happen if we submit to the will of Christ?

We are a new creation, no longer in condemnation, and when we say "Not my will but Yours be done," He gives us the authority to be children of God, which means that we can stand against anything the enemy throws at us – just as Jesus did.

We are in a constant fight with the flesh and so our obedience is an on-going process, sometimes a struggle, sometimes easy. But whatever we may face, we can say with confidence that He has been there before us.

Therefore submit to God. Resist the devil and he will flee from you. Draw near to God and He will draw near to you. James 4:7-8

- If someone tells you to submit to something, do you react badly to it?
- Do you know you have an issue with those in authority over you?
- Have you been abused by people in positions of power?

For some people, submission is really difficult. For others it is easy, and can be a wonderful expression of their love for God. There will also be those who are just confused by the process of guidance and obedience because God seems too far away to be interested.

Whatever your experience of authority in your past, good or bad, be encouraged that submission to the will of God is not another heavy burden that will sap your energy and drain life from your soul.

When you ask God to do His will in your life, you are inviting in the presence of a Father and Friend and Helper as well as the One who has lived through the ultimate obedience and can help you in every single aspect of it as a result. He has tasted it first hand and He loves you so much. You can trust in this authority.

I guarantee it!

Meditate

"Jesus, I want to be honest with you that at times, my expectation when I pray 'Your will be done on earth as it is in Heaven' is that Your will may cause me to become a shadow of who I really am.

It's so easy to think that obedience and submission to You will result in more religious behaviour and less enjoyment of life as You intended it. I don't really know where that mindset came from, because when I think about You and study Your word, I see a God full of love and mercy and encouragement. I would like to encounter the truth again today and leave the trappings of expectation behind. I want my obedience to You to enhance who I am today, not restrict it. I want You to reveal to me how much better life is when I am in the centre of Your will and when I am not motivated by my own selfishness. I'd like to repent of my wrong belief system and I choose to turn around and see You in truth."

"Jesus, I can never fully express how grateful I am that You chose to submit to Your Father, paying the ultimate price so that I could be completely free. You gave me the best gift I could ever be given. Thank you. Amen."

6. Provision

Give us this day our daily bread

It's interesting that right in the middle of The Lord's Prayer, with its focus on the greatness of God and His ultimate authority, comes the sentence, "Give us this day our daily bread." It immediately makes everything more personal and is a cry to God to take care of us and our needs. Why does Jesus choose to say it here? Why didn't He include it at the end after everything else is said? Doesn't it seem a bit out of place?

Much more than bread and butter

To really understand it, we need to dig a bit deeper.

The late John Stott said,

"Luther had the wisdom to see that 'bread' was a symbol for 'everything necessary for the preservation of this life, like food, a healthy body, good weather, house, home, wife, children, good government and peace, and probably we should add that by 'bread' Jesus meant the necessities rather than the luxuries of life." (John R. W. Stott, 1978)

In other words, to pray, "Give us this day our daily bread" is to ask God to supply all our needs, including food, a healthy body, good weather, a home, a spouse, children, good government, and so on. In the first chapter of the book of James we read,

Do not be deceived, my beloved brethren. Every good gift and every perfect gift is from above, and comes down from the Father of lights, with whom there is no variation or shadow of turning. Of His own will He brought us forth by the word of truth, that we might be a kind of first fruits of His creatures. James 1 16-18

We shouldn't reduce God to being the giver of just one or two things! James says we must realise that when we engage God and ask Him for sustenance, we can go to Him about anything at all. He supplies all our needs, whatever they are and as we will see, He is the same in this yesterday, today and forever.

He is an extravagantly generous God and I'm so glad about that aren't you? Does it mean that we get greedy and see Him as a benevolent doddery old man? Not at all, because what we need isn't what someone else needs and vice versa. We mustn't use this prayer as a mantra for our own fleshly desires.

I mix with some people who feel they need to keep up their image by having a new car every six months. Whether I agree with this isn't the issue, but if I adopted the same view, it would just be my greed talking. I don't need a new car every six months. There is value in establishing the difference in our own lives between need and greed and if we don't need, God won't provide. When He provided Abraham a ram in the thicket, it was after a time of interaction between God and Abraham over the sacrifice of Isaac. Abraham's acute need was for a substitute sacrifice and God met his need that day in the form of a ram.

Then Abraham lifted his eyes and looked, and there behind him was a ram caught in a thicket by its horns. So Abraham went and took the ram, and offered it up for a burnt offering instead of his son. Genesis 22:13

Where there's no need, there's no provision.

Manna in the wilderness

It was Jewish custom that only enough food was needed in a home to cater for the needs of each day. It's not like the modern Western culture today where we moan if we don't have a cupboard full of nice things. If a Jewish traveller went on a journey, he would be dependent upon the hospitality of the houses he visited for his food. If there was no food in a home, there was not only a hungry family, but there was also no opportunity to show kindness to the stranger. In the Old Testament, as the Israelites left Egypt, there were no homes to cater for one million refugees who had no food, so God needed to intervene in a special way.

Our fathers ate the manna in the desert; as it is written, 'He gave them bread from heaven to eat.' John 6:31

I'm sure you remember the story, but let me summarise it for you. When the Israelites were wandering in the wilderness without a permanent home, they grumbled and moaned a lot and one of the things they were unhappy about was the lack of food. In response, God sent them His miracle food called manna, which comes from the Hebrew meaning "What is it?" Except on the Sabbath, the fresh bread appeared overnight every day for forty years in order that God's people would never go hungry. If they tried hoarding it, however, it would go bad and start to stink. God doesn't like greed. He prefers it when we rely on Him to supply when we need it.

Supply based on obedience

Every commandment which I command you today you must be careful to observe, that you may live and multiply, and go in and possess the land of which the Lord swore to your fathers. And you shall remember that the Lord your God led you all the way these forty years in the wilderness, to humble you and test you, to know what was in your heart, whether you would keep His commandments or not. So He humbled you, allowed you to hunger, and fed you with manna which you did not know nor did your fathers know, that He might make you know that man shall not live by bread alone; but man lives by every word that proceeds from the mouth of the Lord. Your garments did not wear out on you, nor did your foot swell these forty years. You should know in your heart that as a man chastens his son, so the Lord your God chastens you. Therefore you shall keep the commandments of the Lord your God, to walk in His ways and to fear Him. For the Lord your God is bringing you into a good land, a land of brooks of water, of fountains and springs, that flow out of valleys and hills; a land of wheat and barley, of vines and fig trees and pomegranates, a land of olive oil and honey; a land in which you will eat bread without scarcity, in which you will lack nothing; a land whose stones are iron and out of whose hills you can dig copper. When you have eaten and are full, then you shall bless the Lord your God for the good land which He has given you. Deuteronomy 8:1-10

God is expressing Himself loud and clear. The Israelites lived in His miraculous blessing and provision because He was committed to them, loved them and wanted to protect them – but He also wanted to test their hearts. He wanted to know if they were faithful to Him and whether they would fear Him, keep His commandments and walk in obedience to His ways.

When they did acknowledge their need of Him, God responded by pouring out every kind of blessing on them, including daily manna and clothes that didn't wear out. Not only that, but their feet didn't swell which can only be a good thing in a hot desert!

We must be careful to understand the importance of obedience alongside the provision of God. Have you noticed that, "Give us this day our daily bread" comes immediately after "Your kingdom come, Your will be done on earth as it is in heaven"? We need to remember to honour God first and then put our requests to Him.

It's not a difficult formula. In fact, it's very easy to understand that it's His will before my will; all the time every time. Let me tell you one of my favourite stories to illustrate my point.

You want me to go where?

As a pastor, you have to live what you preach. It's no good telling people about obedience if you're not living a life of obedience yourself. One of the greatest stories of God's provision for my life and my family's life comes from a good few years ago now, but it never ceases to make me praise God for His goodness.

I come from a working class background. As a blue-collar worker, it was difficult for me to get into the white-collar world of management. Amazingly, I had managed to get a breakthrough into the world of pensions and I knew that if I could sell enough policies I could earn enough to pay for the running of the church I had begun to pastor as well as provide for my family.

One day I got a big break. A company in Stoke-on-Trent wanted to see me about a pension scheme and I knew that if I could pull this off, I'd have enough money to do all I needed to do for the month. The only trouble was, the day that the company in Stoke wanted to see me fell during the same week I had booked off to conduct a mission in a poor church in the south of England. I phoned the company and asked a Mr Fox, the man in charge of pensions, if I could possibly move our appointment. He said that was fine and he would phone me shortly to rearrange. Except, of course, he didn't and I resigned myself to losing the contract in order to honour my prior commitment to the church down south. I thought, "God, what have I got myself into? How can that have happened?" It was so near and yet so far!

I didn't tell Molly about any of this because I didn't want to stress her out. I went ahead and did the mission in a church that couldn't afford to pay me anything and I knew I had lost my chance to get into the corporate market. I left the house the following Monday morning, got into my little Morris Minor, and drove around the corner. I had virtually no petrol, no money and no appointments and I just buried my head in my hands and cried. I thought, "I have nowhere to go."

Suddenly I heard the Lord speak to me.

He said, "Essex Street."

I said, "You what?"

He said, "Essex Street."

I didn't know what this meant, but I thought I had better do something, so I began to drive into Birmingham centre – not knowing whether there was an Essex Street or not, but thinking that if it was going to be anywhere it would be in the city itself.

After I had driven around a little bit, I saw a man walking down a street in front of me, so I stopped the car and I asked him if he knew where Essex Street was.

"No," he said, "I'm just visiting here on business. I live in Stoke-on-Trent."

"Oh?" I said, "That's interesting. I was due to be in Stoke last week but I couldn't go as I had another appointment."

"Funny you should say that," he replied. "Last week a man from Birmingham was due to come and have a meeting with me, but he had double booked so had to cancel the appointment."

I said, "Is your name Fox?"

He said, "Is your name Carr?"

It turned out that he was the Mr Fox in charge of pensions at the company I was supposed to visit! Since I was obviously David Carr we decided to head to a restaurant for lunch where we did a deal and I had a month's business just like that! Eventually I found out there is an Essex Street in Birmingham, but it was miles away from where I was. It wasn't important in any case – God just used that to get me driving into the city where He had prearranged this amazing divine appointment.

Do you get it? If I hadn't have been obedient to the voice of God and turned on the ignition to drive, in faith, to a street I had never heard of, I would never have met this guy. God provided for my needs and the needs of my family and church in response to my willingness to honour Him first and also trust His voice.

Give us this day our daily bread.

You want me to do what?

Sometimes, in order to release the blessing, God asks us to do something out of the ordinary. Remember the story of the feeding of the five thousand? It's in every one of the Gospels, which is unusual, so it must be highly significant.

In response to Jesus' request to have the five loaves and two fish brought to him, the disciples were not full of faith. Thousands of hungry people had followed Jesus, eager to hear His teachings and see and experience the miracles He performed. He didn't want to send them away hungry, so when the disciples brought the bread and fish to him, He made it stretch, miraculously! I've seen my wife stretch the food at our table to feed extra mouths, but it would be nothing like this. Not only that, but there were twelve baskets left over – abundant provision.

The disciples knew enough about Jesus by that stage to ever think about ignoring Him. Regardless of how they felt about the imminent possibilities, they expected He would do something spectacular.

Sometimes, God asks us to step out in faith in ways that look silly to those who are observers. He doesn't always make sense and it's not always logical. He will always push the boundaries of our expectation and draw us out of our comfort zone, which may not be comfortable and may feel awkward at times, but that's a life of faith.

Carpet for our feet

You know something of my background now and you'll have picked up that I struggled a lot to provide for my wife and kids in the early days. We managed to get a mortgage in a miraculous way and once we had moved in, even though it was exciting it was also daunting, as we had no furniture back then.

These days, it's fashionable to have stripped wooden floors and people pay a lot of money for the rustic look. Years ago, if you had uncarpeted floorboards, you were poor. It was as simple as that and that is what we had. When she was small, our daughter Melanie used to fall over and get splinters in her knees from the rough wood. All this was at a time when I had promised God I would give a certain amount of time to Him for church work, knowing that the church couldn't afford to pay me. I remember saying to Molly, "If I don't work for the church for a month and earn enough money somewhere else, we can afford to carpet the floor."

I have a wonderful wife. She reminded me of the promise I made to God and how important it was I kept my word to Him and remained obedient. I'm looking at my daughter getting splinters in her knee and wondered how I could make sense of it all and what God would or could do to change such a seemingly small thing.

Then one day I received a phone call from a professional couple in the church. They told us that one of their relatives had died leaving them some money. They told me that the Lord had asked them to buy us a carpet. My instant thought was, "I don't need it, give it to the poor!"

But hang on! I had been asking God for my daily bread and now, when He wanted to provide for me, my own pride was turning it away. I had always found it easier to give than receive, but I could clearly see that here it wasn't out of humility, but pride. I was too proud to receive from others and God wanted to deal with me about it.

The couple went on to tell us that if we didn't choose the best Axminster they would refuse to buy a carpet for us at all. Still I struggled with the thought that we would have a posh carpet when I knew people who didn't have three meals a day. But God challenged me by reminding me that the poor would always be with us and that this gift was between Him and me and He wanted to show Himself as Father and Provider. He had worked in the hearts of our friends in the church to lead me to a place of faith.

I can't tell you how wonderful that carpet was!

Steak for our stomachs

God is always looking for opportunities to bless His children as they trust and obey Him. Two weeks after the carpet incident Molly asked me what food I would like to eat if money was no object.

"Steak," I said. "I haven't had steak for ages."

My business was struggling and some days I could hardly afford petrol, so steak was a real luxury I just used to dream about.

Then one day, I opened our front door to find a bag on the doorstep. Inside it was two enormous pieces of steak! When I went to church that day someone came up to me and said, "I hope you don't think I'm silly, but I was passing a butchers when God spoke to me and said, 'Your pastor needs the best steak you can get, so buy some and go and leave it on his doorstep.'"

She asked me, "Does that make sense to you?"

"Yes," I said wanly.

It's not that I wasn't grateful, I was just incredulous that God would care about blessing me in ways I hadn't even prayed about. I hadn't prayed for two steaks to appear miraculously on my doorstep, I just used to imagine what it was like to eat one! But because I chose to be obedient to God above all else, He answered the prayers I hadn't even prayed yet.

He is that good!

Keep pressing in...

I know people who need something but find it difficult to keep asking God for it because they have been let down in the past. They can't come to terms with the fact that God has not answered their needs immediately, when they feel they have done everything right and so deserve an answer.

My response is, "What's that got to do with you?"

We don't always give our kids what they want when they want it, do we? If we did, some of us would be bankrupt! There is a real difference between need and greed and when we come to God for answers, we have to approach Him as Father. He is the best parent anyone could ever want because He absolutely knows what's best for us. Sometimes we need to be persistent when we ask, but always based on a foundation of trust that He has heard our cry and will answer – even if things don't take shape the way we want them to or think they should.

So I say to you, ask, and it will be given to you; seek, and you will find; knock, and it will be opened to you. For everyone who asks receives, and he who seeks finds, and to him who knocks it will be opened. If a son asks for bread from any father among you, will he give him a stone? Or if he asks for a fish, will he give him a serpent instead of a fish? Or if he asks for an egg, will he offer him a scorpion? If you then, being evil, know how to give good gifts to your children, how much more will your heavenly Father give the Holy Spirit to those who ask Him! Luke 11:9-13

....and keep pressing on

A born-again ex-drunk was once asked, flippantly, if he had ever seen Jesus turn water into wine when he needed it. He replied that he hadn't. But what he had seen was Jesus turn wine into a marriage, a family and a home. The disciples were told to pray "Give us this day our daily bread." Whatever it is we need for today, God can provide for us. Nothing is too difficult for Him.

Charles Haddon Spurgeon put it this way:

"What a serene and quiet life might you lead if you would leave providing to the God of providence! With a little oil in the cruse, and a handful of meal in the barrel, Elijah outlived the famine, and you will do the same. If God cares for you, why need you care too? Can you trust Him for your soul, and not for your body? He has never refused to bear your burdens! He has never fainted under their weight! Come, then, soul! Have done with fretful care, and leave all thy concerns in the hand of a gracious God."

Let it be so.

Time to Reflect

- Do you really believe that if you ask Him, God will supply your daily bread?
- Do you have testimonies of His provision that you could write or speak about? (I guarantee that if you have, you would bless people around you so much!)
- Is there grief and disappointment in you for the prayers you have prayed but not seen answered in the ways you wanted or expected?
- Would you like to reach a new place of faith today? Well, there is no time like the present.

Meditate

There is a famous hymn whose first verse reads,

What a Friend we have in Jesus, all our sins and griefs to bear!
What a privilege to carry everything to God in prayer!
O what peace we often forfeit, O what needless pain we bear,
All because we do not carry everything to God in prayer.
–Joseph M. Scriven

It is such a huge privilege to take everything to God in prayer. He is King of Kings and Lord of Lords, majestic in power and authority and His rule is far above any other. But He is also our Father, our Friend, our Helpmeet, our Guide and the lifter of our heads. He gives us our daily bread and nurtures us physically, emotionally, mentally and spiritually. No situation we face, whatever it is, is too difficult for Him to supply what we need to solve the puzzle. Let Him draw near to you by the presence of His Holy Spirit as we pray together.

"Lord, You have been there for me when I have needed You in the past. I look back and can testify to Your kindness and love so many times and I'm really grateful. It's difficult not to be anxious though, and sometimes I really don't know how things are going to pan out in my life, so I want to be honest with You about that today. Sometimes I've been disappointed because I thought You would answer me in ways that assured me You were listening and when You didn't, I think my heart may have become a little harder towards You as I believed the lies the enemy whispered to me that said You didn't care. I'm sorry about that."

"Lord, my Bible is full of amazing stories of the care You give Your children by meeting their needs in so many wonderful ways. So how can I believe anything different? Why would you change who You are when it comes to me? I know You wouldn't do that, so today I once again choose to take You at Your word and believe that as I lean into You again and recommit my ways into Your ways, You will show Yourself faithful and You will give me my daily bread. Thank you so much. Amen."

7. Forgiveness

And forgive us our debts,
as we forgive our debtors

We have now come to the fascinating section of The Lord's Prayer which introduces the issue of forgiveness. If you do an online search for quotations on this topic you'll see a vast array of statements from all sorts of people who have once spoken or written about what an important thing it is to forgive one another. Mark Twain said, "Forgiveness is the fragrance that the violet sheds on the heel that has crushed it" and C.S Lewis stated that, "To be a Christian means to forgive the inexcusable because God has forgiven the inexcusable in you."

It's not just Christians who believe in the power of forgiveness either. Politicians, philosophers, authors, sportsmen, artists, scientists and film stars are all listed as saying something about it.

"Forgiveness liberates the soul," Nelson Mandela said, "That's why it's such a powerful weapon."

In Matthew's Gospel, Jesus tells His disciples to pray, asking God's forgiveness for their own sin just as they would forgive people who would sin against them. Forgiveness is a two-sided thing: we learn to let go of what's been done against us just as God lets go of all we do that hurts Him.

But how can we keep forgiving when at times it's just so tough? It all goes back to the Old Testament.

The place of honour

Honour your father and your mother, that your days may be long upon the land which the Lord our God is giving you. Exodus 20:12

At the beginning of the creation of the nation of Israel, God issued Ten Commandments to Moses by which His people would live their lives. They weren't just good ideas or petty rules, they reflected God's heart for His people because they needed boundaries in place for their lives to be fruitful, fulfilling and peaceful.

The commandment to honour our father and mother was God's way of ensuring that grace would flow between generations. If there is no honour for those who have gone before, the foundations on which we build our own lives are shaky and self-centred. God promises His people that where there is a commitment to honour, the individual who lives that way will, as a certain Vulcan once said, live long and prosper!

It really does matter how we treat our parents. Most people don't realise that it has implications on their spiritual wellbeing. By "honouring" I don't mean that if, for instance, they are cruel and abusive we can't distance ourselves to prevent further bad treatment. Honour is more than just obedience, it is an attitude and a choice. What God wants is that our hearts are open to honour our parents, forgiving them regardless of what has happened in life. In doing that very thing, it is we who will benefit and our lives that will flourish as we experience the blessing of God.

Blessed is he whose transgression is forgiven,
Whose sin is covered.
Blessed is the man to whom the Lord does not impute iniquity,
And in whose spirit there is no deceit. Psalms 32:1-2

My father, my inspiration

When I think about the honour my father showed to his parents, it makes me cry. His mother, my grandmother, was a very difficult and harsh woman who struggled to be a good role model for my Dad. There are countless stories of cruelty and rejection coming from his growing up years which pull at my heartstrings even now. Stories like when he had left home, he walked five miles from his house to her house to pay her a visit, only to find that she would see him coming down the road and often refuse to open the door to him, so he had to walk all the way home again. When he was destined for a successful career which would have made him very rich, she obstructed every opportunity he was given to progress and sent him instead to be a tradesman at Cadbury where he stayed for the rest of his working life without complaint.

Dad wasn't a Christian in those days, but when he was at school he had been taught Christian values. Every day the pupils would say The Lord's Prayer together. I really believe that something was deposited in his soul because of it, which helped him live his life the way he did even before he knew Jesus personally. He used to tell people who asked him why he continued to walk five miles to see his parents only to be rebuffed, that if the Bible said to honour your father and mother that was all there was to it.

One day, years later when I was about to set off for a meeting in Coventry, my sixty-year old Dad fell ill while he was pottering in his garden. Mum phoned me to say Dad was worried he had severe indigestion, but I was a little more suspicious so I raced over there and as soon as I saw him, I knew he was having a coronary.

Dad had never been to hospital in his life up to that point and getting him there was like the battle of David and Goliath, but eventually we persuaded him to go and while we were in casualty, he had a massive heart attack. Had we not taken him, he would certainly have died at home.

So it was that at the age of sixty my Dad gave his life to Jesus. He lived happily for another eighteen years, writing poetry and going along to his local church in Stirchley until he finally left his earthly garden for his heavenly garden full of the presence of God.

I believe God gave my Dad eighteen more years because he had made the choice to honour his father and mother. He had forgiven his parents again and again for the things they had done to him that could have caused him to get bitter and twisted and make his own children's lives a living hell. But he didn't and God blessed him with a longer life full of peace.

'Honour your father and mother,' which is the first commandment with promise:' that it may be well with you and you may live long on the earth.' Ephesians 6:2-3

Are you willing to forgive?

The Lord's Prayer tells us to sort out our own forgiveness issues with God before we pray for those who have hurt us. In other words, to forgive others we have to be wiling to receive God's forgiveness for our own sin. There must be a willingness to encounter it before we are able to administer it.

Are you getting it?

Grace and mercy that flow from a forgiving heart are attributes of the nature of God. Even if someone is not walking with God, they still can live in the flow of His goodness. In the natural, when a crime has been committed, the victim can't find the resources to forgive, as the injustice and pain can be so heavy that it crushes any attempt to overcome it. When we pray "Forgive us our debts as You forgive our debtors", whether we count ourselves as Christians or not, we are willingly giving God permission to forgive us so that we can, in turn, find the strength to forgive people who have hurt us. Didn't my Dad illustrate this perfectly? Isn't it amazing that after praying The Lord's Prayer every day at school and even before He was a Christian he was still able to forgive his parents?

Forgiveness is not...

To forgive is not about being nice to someone on the surface but having a murderous heart underneath. The word forgive means "to grant a pardon or remission". It means to give up all claims to an account that gives someone the right to be offended. Sometimes people fear that if they forgive someone it means they get off scot free and all the bad things that have happened are suddenly neutralised, so the only way to remember the injustice is to grip onto it.

I remember a woman coming to talk with me at the end of a service once about a man who had accidentally killed her young child and she had not been able to forgive him. Year by year she was getting more and more embittered and her life was bound up by the anger and pain of the injustice of it all. The fact is that this woman was unable to move on from this accident. The man would eventually be released from prison and start his life again, but this woman was destined for a life defined by something that was beyond anyone's control. She told me that by not forgiving him she was going some way towards inflicting the same pain on him as he had inflicted on her. But it wasn't working that way, because in reality she was destroying herself. Sad isn't it?

Forgiveness is...

To forgive someone sets us free to allow God to judge the situation that has ripped us to pieces and deal with the perpetrator in His own way and in His own time. It's about trusting that He understands our pain and anger and wants to take it on Himself. God didn't create us to be crushed under the weight of burdens of unforgiveness. He made us to be free from such burdens and that is what the cross is all about.

The cry of the cross

Come and stand at the cross with me and see what happened.
Then Jesus said, 'Father, forgive them, for they do not know what they do.' Luke 23:34

Jesus' journey to the cross and the ultimate sacrifice He made for mankind was a fulfilment of the words of the prophet Isaiah spoken centuries before:

For He was cut off from the land of the living;
For the transgressions of My people He was stricken.
And they made His grave with the wicked
But with the rich at His death,
Because He had done no violence,
Nor was any deceit in His mouth.
Yet it pleased the Lord to bruise Him;
He has put Him to grief. Isaiah 53:8b-10

The cry of Jesus to His Father, asking Him to forgive those who crucified Him, preceded the plea of the thief on the cross next to Him. This man was dying for his own crimes and was staring into the mouth of hell. It was following Jesus' act of free will to forgive that opened the way for the thief to seek forgiveness.

There was no way this criminal could have been forgiven had Jesus not offered him the opportunity. For the first time, at the point of death, this man knew that he had an assurance of paradise. That one cry of Jesus not only opened the way for generations to come, but it was a personal invitation for the two men hanging beside Jesus to accept the offer of eternal life. What a tragedy that only one of them took it!

Somebody had to make the first move. It's always that way with forgiveness. I've heard people say that they would forgive the person who did them wrong if only they would make the first move, but Jesus modelled it a different way. At the point when His suffering must have been off the scale, He still put others first and made the ultimate first move.

In the same way, Jesus' cry on the cross revealed to a Roman centurion that He was the Son of God:

So when the centurion and those with him, who were guarding Jesus, saw the earthquake and the things that had happened, they feared greatly, saying, 'Truly this was the Son of God!' Matthew 27:54

And to a rich Jew who went on to offer his grave for the body of God's Son:

Now when evening had come, there came a rich man from Arimathea, named Joseph, who himself had also become a disciple of Jesus. This man went to Pilate and asked for the body of Jesus. Then Pilate commanded the body to be given to him. When Joseph had taken the body, he wrapped it in a clean linen cloth, and laid it in his new tomb which he had hewn out of the rock; and he rolled a large stone against the door of the tomb, and departed. Matthew 27:57-60

Jesus never allowed unforgiveness to invade His spirit because He was without sin. But His statement in The Lord's Prayer begins with a request for God to come and forgive our own sin first, so that it enables us to release forgiveness to others. We can't do one without first doing the other! As we reach out to Him, He enables us to both experience forgiveness and express forgiveness.

Nobody said it was easy

Some people have to face the most horrendous circumstances in their lives through no fault of their own, and yet have learned that forgiveness is the best way. During the conflict in Northern Ireland, so many acts of violence were perpetrated in the name of freedom that fear, anger and suspicion were never far from the surface. It was a case of one murder deserving another and retaliation triumphing over mercy.

Except it didn't always happen like that.

I remember how when a nurse was blown up by an IRA bomb, her father, a Christian, held her hand in her final few moments as she said, "I love you Daddy." As he buried his daughter, this man, who had every reason to seek revenge and become bitter, decided he would forgive the people who had taken his beloved daughter away from him. Eventually, he became a politician in the Republican parliament and was honoured for the strong choice he had made.

What a witness to the power of forgiveness.

The wife of the deputy governor of the Maze prison had one day eaten breakfast with her husband and seen him cuddle their baby before he went to the front door to leave to drive to work. As he opened it he was gunned down by four masked gunmen. As she knelt down by her dead husband, all she could remember was the moisture of his last kiss, still on her lips.

She told me as I interviewed her for a television programme, that as a Christian she knew she needed to forgive these men because if she didn't, she too would have died with her husband that day. So that was the choice she made in the most terrible of circumstances. I remember asking her if she got angry about what had happened. "Of course I do!" she replied. She went on to speak of her regret that these men, who were serving long prison sentences, could not live their lives replacing some of the things her husband used to do that she no longer could, like cutting the hedges or painting the house. What a marvellous woman!

What a witness to the power of forgiveness!

Another interview I did was with a lovely Catholic couple whose one and only son had studied at Queens University, got married, had a baby son and was working as a taxi driver to make ends meet. One night he found himself in the wrong part of the divide and a group of men dragged him from his car shooting him twice in the head, killing him instantly. At the time he was shot, his parents were holidaying in their caravan and, on hearing the news, the father ran down the beach screaming, "They've killed my boy!" Suddenly, the man heard an audible voice which said. "Yes, they did that to mine as well."

The father ran back to his wife and told her that they had to choose to forgive the men who did this to their son, otherwise they would die. They even went on television to state that they had forgiven the Protestants who had left them without a son and his wife without a father for their child.

This is the power of forgiveness!

Only God can help people forgive like that. It is not easy being a Christian and it is not easy to forgive – but it is not impossible, and when we choose it, it brings life and reconciliation that is at the heart of the cross.

Nobody said it was unconditional

The parable of the unforgiving servant in Matthew 18 teaches us that salvation is free, but it is not unconditional. When his merciful and forgiving master released the servant from the unpayable debt he owed, he should have responded by showing the same mercy to one of the other servants, but he failed to do so.

But that servant went out and found one of his fellow servants who owed him a hundred denarii; and he laid hands on him and took him by the throat, saying, 'Pay me what you owe!' Matthew 18:28

When the master heard about what had happened, he threw the servant to the torturers until he could pay the debt.

So My heavenly Father also will do to you if each of you, from his heart, does not forgive his brother his trespasses. Matthew 18:35

Jesus is crystal clear here and He is very serious indeed. Forgiveness is not an option. As Christians we have received complete and unconditional forgiveness from the One who has settled our debt once and for all. What a relief!

I want to challenge you now, in response to that wonderful gift, that you can't not extend the same mercy to your brothers and sisters.

God takes it seriously when we are conditional with aspects of salvation He has given us freely, and He will respond to our stubbornness with action. He is not mocked; make no mistake about it.

Let forgiveness flow!

In our churches we will have feuds and arguments, relationship breakdowns and betrayals. Let's be real about it because we spend so much of our time trying to be good, we lose our grip on the reality of what is really going on under the surface.

In 1 Corinthians 11 Paul writes about the importance of dealing with issues of unforgiveness before taking communion and the consequences for the individual should it not be sorted:

For he who eats and drinks in an unworthy manner eats and drinks judgment to himself, not discerning the Lord's body. 1 Corinthians 11:29

He even goes on to say that some people are sick in the Corinthian church because of unforgiveness, and some of them have even died before their allotted time because of it.

Scripture also teaches us to approach the person who is in need of our forgiveness, to point out their faults. If he doesn't listen, there will need to be one or two other people called in and if that fails, then it is appropriate to then tell it to the church elders who will exercise their authority and governance over the matter.

God did not send Jesus to die for a Church full of arguing, bickering people driven by unforgiveness and judgement. No! Let's not get too spiritual and high and mighty about this. We just need to get on and forgive one another. We need to stop telling God and others what wrong has been done to us and expect the other party to make the first move. Forgiveness is costly, yes, but we harm ourselves more if we refuse to forgive. When we do, however, it will release the sweet aroma of the brokenness of Christ's death back into His body, repairing it and restoring its beauty.

"He that cannot forgive others breaks the bridge over which he must pass himself; for every man has need to be forgiven." (Thomas Fuller)

By forgiving someone we do not validate the perpetrator, but we release ourselves from the imprisonment of the violation.

Calvary was the innocent sacrificing for the guilty. If you know God has forgiven you as you read this, then make a choice to forgive the person or people who are still crushed under the weight of your harsh judgement. I'm not making light of the circumstances each of us have faced or will face in the future – some things perpetrated against us are just too horrid for words – but that is where the cross comes in.

Did Jesus die for only the favoured few? No!

Does the work of the cross cover any and every evil thing that has been said and done against you? Yes!

We have all needed forgiveness at some time in our lives and so with the measure that we have been given it we are required to give it away to others. I have had to forgive past members of my church who, years ago, would write me letters so abusive I could hardly bear to open them. If I did have the courage to see what was inside I would flip to the last page to see how the letter was worded at the end and if it contained a "We love you Pastor" I knew I could stop sweating a bit and carefully read through the rest of it.

There has been a lot of hurt over the years, but the more I forgave, the easier it became. Don't get me wrong, I'm not the personification of virtue, far from it! But something definitely happens when you choose the Christlike qualities laid bare on the cross. The Holy Spirit takes up more room inside your heart and you begin to change.

Why not give it a go?

Time to Reflect

- Do you remember a time when someone forgave you for something?
- Can you remember how it felt?
- Have you struggled with forgiving yourself over an unresolved issue?

- Is the guilt and shame crushing you?
- Would you like to be set free from it?
- Finally, think about who you need to forgive and why. Remember that you are holding that person in bondage with your harsh judgement of them, and it really is God's job to deal with the issues in their life that caused them to hurt you the way they did.

There are always reasons not to forgive someone. People can be so unkind (whether they mean to be or not) that we hold onto the hurt, scared that we will never see the justice restored into the situation. We don't want them to escape the punishment for their wrongdoing and we feel it is up to us to keep our anger with them present all the time. We can doubt that God is able to help or would even fight on our behalf.

The truth is, forgiving someone is a strong thing to do. Handing the situation over to God is not admitting defeat, it is rejoicing in victory. When we do it, the whole of Heaven gives a massive cheer as everybody wins! God then gets to work repairing the damage, healing the heart and restoring the soul and He is very very good at it. Let's pray.

"Father, I need Your help to forgive (insert any names here from the past or present, including your own). In an ideal world none of this stuff would have happened and I would not need to dig deep today to find the strength to admit I have to forgive. What I do know, though, is that I wouldn't be who I am today unless you had met me. Jesus, the cross takes my breath away. Your cry, "Father forgive them.." echoes down the centuries and into my own world today as I remember that You forgave me first. There is nothing I can do that You can't and won't forgive and I'm amazed by Your kindness to me. I want to cherish Your sacrifice not dishonour it. I'm sorry that I can think of millions of excuses not to forgive someone, when You likely had so many more reasons not to forgive me. So today, will you meet me and lead me back to the cross where it all changed? Will you please fill me with the same Spirit that lived in You so that I can walk in the same power? I want to be free from the tight ropes of unforgiveness that bind, so I choose to give you everything now. Thank you. Amen."

8. Temptation & Deliverance

And do not lead us into temptation...

When Jesus told His disciples to pray that the Father would not lead them into temptation, I wonder if they stopped to think about how confusing a concept that sounded? Was Jesus implying that God could actually lead them into something bad or destructive? Does God tempt us? If God is wholly perfect and perfectly good, as the Bible teaches us and we know from experience, then surely God is unable to do that, isn't He?

What does Jesus mean here?

In the gospel accounts of Jesus' temptation in the wilderness, it's clear from the start that He was led into the desert by the Holy Spirit to face Satan, whose only aim was to coax Jesus into sin. Tested to the limits of His endurance, Jesus nevertheless overcame the enemy's strategy not once but three times. After the final time, it was clear the battle was won.

Then Jesus said to him, 'Away with you, Satan! For it is written, "You shall worship the Lord your God, and Him only you shall serve."' Then the devil left Him, and behold, angels came and ministered to Him. Matthew 4:1-11

Jesus' righteousness was proven through the trials He faced and He was led into that place for that very reason. God will sometimes do that with you and me. It isn't pleasant and it isn't something I would necessarily pray for. But it is God's way of focussing us on what is important by leading us to nail our colours to the mast. Because of God's favour towards us and in time, just like with Jesus, the enemy will leave us alone as His presence comes to soothe our battle weary souls.

Let me make it clear: when God allows us to be tempted to test us, it will be very different from being led by the enemy into disobedience and rebellion. The former will have positive results, the latter only negative. We will look at that a bit more as we go through this chapter.

But let's delve deeper into understanding how Jesus handled temptation.

The wilderness and the garden

For we do not have a High Priest who cannot sympathize with our weaknesses, but was in all points tempted as we are, yet without sin. Hebrews 4:15

Come with me to the searing heat of the desert in the Palestine of Jesus' day. Jesus has just been baptised by John in the River Jordan and heard his Father speak tender words over Him and felt the Holy Spirit rest on Him. It could have been easy after that and Jesus could have started His ministry from there, but instead He was led into the wilderness where He fasted from food for forty days and nights. Vulnerable and weak, the enemy then sidles up to Him and challenges Him to make bread from stones. Jesus answers Him, saying,

It is written, 'Man shall not live by bread alone, but by every word that proceeds from the mouth of God.' Matthew 4:4

Twice more the enemy tries it on, and twice more Jesus resists him using words from Scripture. Jesus had to be tempted in every way so that all humanity would know there was no temptation He had gone through that He hadn't also resisted.

In the cool of the Garden of Gethsemane, towards the end of His life, Jesus was under so much pressure to give in to the temptation to back away from the suffering ahead of Him that He sweated drops of blood – an indication of extreme stress.

And being in agony, He prayed more earnestly. Then His sweat became like great drops of blood falling down to the ground. Luke 22:44

What human being with any sense would want to die the cruelest death ever invented? Two thousand years on, there is still no death worse than crucifixion, and yet Jesus submitted His own will to the will of His Father and went through with it for you and me. Aren't you glad He overcame the temptation to wimp out? Hallelujah, what a Saviour!

Both times, Jesus fulfilled the test of righteousness and conquered the temptation of Satan to unrighteousness. The request, lead us not into temptation, is really a heart cry for the Holy Spirit to continue to lead us into all righteousness and not leave us alone when we face the temptation of the enemy. The truth is, of course, that while God may well test us out of His love for us, to prove our righteousness, He will never abandon us when we face the lure of unrighteousness.

The mountain and the ram

Now it came to pass after these things that God tested Abraham, and said to him, 'Abraham!' And he said, 'Here I am.' Then He said,

'Take now your son, your only son Isaac, whom you love, and go to the land of Moriah, and offer him there as a burnt offering on one of the mountains of which I shall tell you.' Genesis 22:1-2

I want you to picture Abraham. Here is a man who had been praying for a son which would make sense of the prophecies given to him years ago by God, that he would be a "father of many". As he and his wife Sarah had grown old, the chance of them conceiving naturally had gone, so in desperation Abraham slept with a slave who bore him a son, Ishmael; born illegitimately and outside of God's promise. Eventually however, Sarah conceives and Isaac is born, who is the fulfilment of the promise.

Years later, God tells Abraham to take his son to the top of a mountain and sacrifice him there. As they travel together, Isaac asks why there is no lamb for the burnt offering and Abraham responds:

My son, God will provide for Himself the lamb for a burnt offering. Genesis 22:8

Abraham got so far as tying Isaac with ropes, laying him on the wood of the altar and drawing his knife ready to kill him, when God suddenly called out to him to stop and replace Isaac with a ram that had got caught in a bush nearby.

And He said, 'Do not lay your hand on the lad, or do anything to him; for now I know that you fear God, since you have not withheld your son, your only son, from Me.' Genesis 22:12

God had tested Abraham to the limit and there was no doubt he would have gone through with the sacrifice in order to obey God. Hebrews chapter 11 commends him for his faith and trust in the purposes of God even when everything was confusing and God seemed to be contradicting His promise.

By faith Abraham obeyed when he was called to go out to the place which he would receive as an inheritance. And he went out, not knowing where he was going. Hebrews 11:8

Temptation versus testing

I want to make a clear distinction between temptation and testing. We all have strengths and we all have weaknesses. The Apostle Paul is very clear about this in Galatians, writing that it is a constant battle to bring his flesh under submission to the Spirit.

For the flesh lusts against the Spirit, and the Spirit against the flesh; and these are contrary to one another, so that you do not do the things that you wish. Galatians 5:17

If a person struggled with alcohol addiction you wouldn't offer them a glass of wine would you? If you know an active drug addict, it's very unlikely you would recommend them as a drug counsellor isn't it? Whoever we are, we all have weaknesses and a predilection towards something that wants to control us. This is the flesh that Paul is talking about and it is constantly at war with the freedom the Spirit brings. The enemy will take every opportunity to tempt each of us into giving way to our flesh so that we are bound by guilt and shame. Let me reiterate: God does not tempt us in this way.

In Matthew's gospel, Jesus warns His disciples to,

Watch and pray, lest you enter into temptation. The spirit indeed is willing, but the flesh is weak. Matthew 26:41

Watching is quite simply keeping our eyes open to the areas in our lives that are vulnerable to temptation. And these are not just the weak areas either! It's often our strengths that can be our Achilles heel too. Think about it: if someone is leading a church which has seen a sudden surge of miracles and signs and wonders after years of praying for them and people come from far and wide to get a taste of it, how easy is it for that leader to begin to swell with pride? What is happening around him can easily become about him! Temptation is always there: watch and pray.

Testing is different. Why? Because its source is different. It comes from God who was prepared to put Jesus and Abraham, as well as many others in the Bible and since, through circumstances that have the potential for great victory or great defeat. It's not done out of cruelty, but out of love and a desire for relationship, as this verse indicates:

So He humbled you, allowed you to hunger, and fed you with manna which you did not know nor did your fathers know, that He might make you know that man shall not live by bread alone; but man lives by every word that proceeds from the mouth of the Lord. Deuteronomy 8:3

Many years ago we had a spilt in our church and 40% of the congregation left in one month. It was horrendous. In the following week, someone rang me and offered me the job of leading a church of five hundred in a beautiful coastal area far away from the smog of Solihull. Who would have blamed me for jumping ship? I knew I could lead those people and part of me just wanted to get away from the pain of what had happened.

But God had already told me that I was to never leave Solihull and however tempting the prospect was to start over, I knew it was not from Him. He was testing my heart. Was I going to give in and settle for an easier life by the sea or was I going to stay faithful to His call and stay put? I stayed put and passed the test and the irony is I am more fulfilled because of it.

Remember what God has spoken into your life because His words won't suddenly change even if your circumstances do.

Biblical scholars McClintock and Strong give four descriptions of temptation, referring to it as deception, infection, seduction and perdition.

- Deception is everywhere in or society and, sadly, often in the Church too. It is what happened in the Garden of Eden when Eve took the fruit after the snake promised her it would make her like God. It takes simple truth and twists it into something that looks attractive, but is destructive, and will often have far reaching consequences. Chapter 6 of Paul's letter to the Ephesians encourages us to stand firm against the deceptive wiles of the enemy, ready to speak truth at all times.
- Infection occurs when a thought takes root and germinates. King David didn't commit adultery on his first date, he became infected with lust over time. The result was not just adultery but murder and the birth of an illegitimate son.
- Seduction says, "Come, come, come…" The object of our affection whispers quietly to us and we believe we will never be truly fulfilled unless we have it, no matter what the cost. It could be a car, a holiday, someone else's partner, or anything. Delilah was the ultimate seducer and the cost to Samson was high indeed.
- Perdition is what happens when a person or group of people give themselves to evil. Some temptation will lead to the most barbaric acts, many of them premeditated and planned. Whether the perpetrators are deceived into believing they are doing the "right thing" or not, there is no reference or justification for what one human being can do to another.

The Bible tells us we are all made in God's image and so everyone has the capacity to live life reflecting His character. The pollution of the soul comes from an external source bent on destruction and we are told to watch out for it. So don't get lazy and think you are exempt because you are not.

Be sober, be vigilant; because your adversary the devil walks about like a roaring lion, seeking whom he may devour. 1 Peter 5:8

Deliver me from evil

Having said all that, just being careful and watching out isn't enough: we need God to deliver us from evil. In 1738 the great hymn writer and preacher Charles Wesley wrote,

Long my imprisoned spirit lay
Fast bound in sin and nature's night.
Thine eye diffused a quickening ray
I woke, the dungeon flamed with light.
My chains fell off, my heart was free
I rose went forth and followed Thee!

And for centuries since, it has been sung heartily by Christians who believe what the Bible says: there is no condemnation for those in Christ Jesus (Romans 8:1). In other words, the freedom offered by Jesus makes the chains that keep us in bondage to sin fall off so they possess no more power over us. Praise God!

In his letter to the Romans, the apostle Paul is honest about his own struggle with sin when he writes about how he desperately wants to do good but he ends up doing the very opposite. He knows that despite his own best efforts, it is not the law that saves him, but the grace of God in Christ Jesus, and if he tries to fight the temptations of the flesh in a natural way, it's hopeless and he ends up looking just like he did before he received Christ.

Living free in Jesus means letting the Spirit of change the way I think and letting go of the control that makes me want to try and overcome things my way. I don't like the words of the song "My

Way" much because it's not about me, it's all about Him. I want to do it "His way." Do you?

If a person is dying and the doctor comes into the hospital ward one morning and says "Guess what! You're not going to die because we have just found a cure for what you've got and I'm going to inject it into your arm so you can go home at lunchtime to be reunited with your family", imagine how ecstatic they would be. Well, we have been delivered from sin and death in the same way! It's time to get excited about what God has done once again. Don't let misery take you over. If you have received Christ you are a new creation, the old has gone forever and eternity awaits!

And the Lord will deliver me from every evil work and preserve me for His heavenly kingdom. To Him be glory forever and ever. Amen! 2 Timothy 4:18

God has delivered you from your old nature and from every evil work that comes out of temptation. He has given you the ultimate cure and you carry it with you every day, so that when any weapon comes against you, it will not prosper (Isaiah 54:17). I'm always grateful I can say to Jesus "I'm in a real mess here" and He answers me with "It's OK. I know how to sort it."

How do I know this?

- He gave Himself. The work of the cross was the ultimate gift for you and me. Jesus has been there, seen it and done it and overcame any work of the enemy which would try to gain authority over us. In Him, it never can, ever again.
- He overcame death. The resurrection delivered Jesus from the grave and has also delivered us from the grave. Who else can deliver us from death? Buddha? Confucius? Mohammed? No! Only Jesus.
- He delivered us from this present age. We may think we have

things bad now, but I can take you back to when our nation was at war with itself during the reign of Charles the first. Things were pretty bad then too. But whatever the age, we are citizens of heaven and we are free from the burdens of having to conform to the godless societies in which we live.

- He has hidden us. "For you died, and your life is hidden with Christ in God" (Colossians 3:3). We are not just delivered and left in a vacuum because He is our shelter in the storm, our hiding place. Whatever we face, we can run to the safety of His protective care and He will shield us from harm.

Fill me with faith

The English writer John Ruskin once wrote,

"Out of suffering comes the serious mind; out of salvation, the grateful heart; out of endurance, fortitude; out of deliverance, faith."

Deliverance from evil builds our faith more than anything else. The God who has the power to deliver one million people out of bondage in Egypt is the same God who can deliver us from habits, addictions, selfishness and unforgiveness.

By faith they passed through the Red Sea as by dry land, whereas the Egyptians, attempting to do so, were drowned. Hebrews 11:29

Our God who raised Jesus from the dead, delivering Him from the grave, is the same God who can deliver you and me from whatever it is that seeks to destroy us.

When we taste true freedom, we tend to want more of it. As we submit to the work of the Holy Spirit who cleans us up from the inside out and puts us back on track, it honestly feels really good. It lifts our eyes and it encourages us to press on in faith for more.

Are you in faith for God to lead you away from temptation and deliver you from evil? Let's take some time now to do some business with God.

Time to Reflect

It may be that in reading this chapter you have become aware of some areas of your life that need the touch of God. Maybe over the years you have slipped into thought patterns or behaviour patterns that are at odds with your outward expression of faith. It's tough to live that way. Perhaps you have felt oppressed and you don't know why. You know that freedom is yours but somehow you feel crushed under a big weight of something and you need God to deliver you. Think for a moment.

- How would it feel to be completely free?
- How would it feel to be completely clean?
- How would it feel to be completely forgiven?

Meditate

God is not surprised by anything. Nothing we do or say or think will shock Him or make Him recoil in disgust. That's because His love for us is deeper than the oceans, higher than the mountains and wider than the whole earth. Nothing can ever or will ever separate us from this love and He will never condemn us because in Christ there is no condemnation. He likes nothing more than to take the guilt and shame and fear away, breaking their hold on our lives and setting us free to enjoy life in all it's fullness. You and I are not the enemy of God, we are His children and He longs to pour out blessing, goodness, forgiveness, grace, mercy and love over us. Are you ready to choose freedom over bondage?

"Father, in the past I have won battles with temptation with Your help and I am so grateful to You for coming to my rescue when I needed it. But like Paul, I am aware of the struggles with my flesh and even though I desire to do good, sometimes I am overwhelmed by the opposite desires. I don't find it very easy to approach You at times because I fear Your judgment of me, but I know that that is a tactic of the enemy to keep me away from You. So today, I would like to bash through all that and boldly approach Your throne to claim my freedom. I will never get over what You have done for me, but I'm not going to make that a reason to become humble in a fake way. I will gladly and gratefully take what You offer me, amazed by Your grace! So deliver me my Lord. Put my feet back on track, dust me down and walk with me again on my journey through life. I love you. Thank you. Amen."

9. Authority & Power

For yours is the kingdom and the power

It is interesting to note that the word "kingdom" is mentioned twice in The Lord's Prayer. Why is that? It's not as if the prayer is very long. Nor is it that this is the only theme that could be repeated. What is so important about God's kingdom that Jesus told His disciples to pray about it twice?

Kingdom invitation

The first time Jesus mentions God's kingdom, it's all to do with calling out for His will to be done. It's no good having power and authority if we don't know who is the source of it, or what it looks like. If we, as God's people, are to live in the reality of His kingdom presence on earth there needs to be a direction, purpose and substance to it, so that everyone can understand it and participate in it.

In the early part of The Lord's Prayer the statement Your kingdom come, Your will be done clearly states who is in charge.

It is His will we are after; it is the perfect rule of heaven that gives structure to the power and authority we are given by the Holy Spirit.

So we invite the kingdom to come. It's a kingdom without anarchy where everything is in perfect order and everything that should work does work. It's a kingdom where those things that don't work simply don't exist.

Have you ever said, "With the best will in the world it will never happen"? Sometimes we want to see change. It could be that we are after a job promotion, a new house, a life partner, a child of our own, but no matter how hard we try, or how earnestly we hope, we know that naturally speaking, for whatever reason, we won't see a positive result.

When an oppressed people group rises up against a despot or dictator things don't often end well. That's because whilst the people have a will and desire for change, they don't have the power and authority necessary to structure or implement it. The result is anarchy.

When we are told to pray the words Your kingdom come, Your will be done, we are inviting the presence of God and His perfect will to settle with us and live among us.

Isn't it great when the will of God is on earth? I love it!

Kingdom application

For Yours is the kingdom and the power. Matthew 6:13b

The shift now comes with the second mention of "kingdom" towards the end of The Lord's Prayer. Jesus combines the use of kingdom (the place where God's will is done) with power. In other words, we can't ever separate the kingdom of God from the power of God – the two have to work hand in hand. That's what gets people healed and set free; that's what changes lives forever! In God, it can never be with the best will in the world it will never happen... because God is not of this world. His kingdom is on a whole new level in which things happen that go beyond the fleshly expectations we have.

I want to see people healed, don't you? But I can't do it on my own. I need the power and the authority in the Holy Spirit that flows from the will of God to heal. Trying to act without the Holy Spirit's power is like expecting a car to run without fuel; it just doesn't work. Miracles don't happen unless the power of the Holy Spirit comes to fill the space.

This application of Jesus' kingdom principles is set clearly in Scripture. Just before He ascended to heaven, Jesus spoke to His disciples saying,

'All authority has been given to Me in heaven and on earth. Go therefore and make disciples of all the nations, baptizing them in the name of the Father and of the Son and of the Holy Spirit, teaching them to observe all things that I have commanded you; and lo, I am with you always, even to the end of the age.' Amen. Matthew 28:18-20

But it didn't stop when Jesus left, of course. He didn't decide to go up in a blaze of glory and let the people of the day just remember the amazing things He did, never to access those things for themselves. No! Read what He said to His disciples in the gospel of John:

Most assuredly, I say to you, he who believes in Me, the works that I do he will do also; and greater works than these he will do, because I go to My Father. John 14:12

All power and authority is given to you and me in His Name, so that His will can be done on His earth.

From authority comes power

In a worldly sense, power often denotes authority. The Prime Minister of the United Kingdom wouldn't be able to introduce new policies of governance if he didn't hold the position he does at the top of the ministerial pile. It is his office as Prime Minister that enables him to act with authority.

In Christ, it works the other way around. Jesus had power because He first had authority, which was given to Him by the Father after He was obedient to the point of death.

And being found in appearance as a man, He humbled Himself and became obedient to the point of death, even the death of the cross. Therefore God also has highly exalted Him and given Him the name which is above every name, that at the name of Jesus every knee should bow, of those in heaven, and of those on earth, and of those under the earth, and that every tongue should confess that Jesus Christ is Lord, to the glory of God the Father. Philippians 2:8-11

In the same way, as Christians we also have His power and authority because we are citizens of the Kingdom of God and we come under His rule and reign. Not only that but, rather than dictating His will to us from an unknown or remote place, God comes with us. He loves His world so much that He sent His Son to die for it, but He also gave us His Holy Spirit to help us live like Jesus lived once He had gone back to be with His Father.

God is relational and He prefers it when He is right in the middle of the action, changing situations and lives for the better. If we invite Him to, the Holy Spirit will partner with us in our everyday lives in a dynamic and powerful way, teaching us how to live like Jesus did. Without the Holy Spirit we can do nothing extraordinary but with the Holy Spirit we are dynamite!

Explosive power

But you shall receive power when the Holy Spirit has come upon you; and you shall be witnesses to Me in Jerusalem, and in all Judea and Samaria, and to the end of the earth. Acts 1:8

In this verse, the word "power" comes from the original Greek dunamis which is used 120 times in the New Testament. It describes a "divine energy" or, as the scholar William MacDonald says, it is when "Unlimited strength is at our disposal. Through the enabling of the Holy Spirit, the believer can serve valiantly, endure patiently, suffer triumphantly, and, if need be, die gloriously."

It is from this Greek word dunamis that we get the word dynamite. When I first read that, it grasped my heart. When the inventors of dynamite wanted to name it – a substance powerful enough to explode through obstacles in its way, destroying that which is bad or opening up that which is good – they chose a word with the same root as the word used for the power of God!

On the day of Pentecost, as a group of people huddled together waiting for something they had been promised, they didn't know what to expect. Would the Holy Spirit come gently, seeping in under the door? Would He appear as a cloud? How would it feel? Then suddenly, BANG! The world witnessed its first dunamis.

When the Day of Pentecost had fully come, they were all with one accord in one place. And suddenly there came a sound from heaven, as of a rushing mighty wind, and it filled the whole house where they were sitting. Then there appeared to them divided tongues, as of fire, and one sat upon each of them. And they were all filled with the Holy Spirit and began to speak with other tongues, as the Spirit gave them utterance. Acts 2:1-4

Things would never be the same again: God had sent His Holy Spirit as an envoy from heaven to live on earth forever from that point on. There was no going back now.

Not only that, but this power is freely and generously given. There are no half measures, no power games, and there is no favouritism. Notice in the verse above that they were all filled; no one was left out.

Do you ever think you are outside the camp when it comes to receiving the Holy Spirit? Do you feel unworthy because there are things you have done or thought or said in the past that disqualify you from receiving the beautiful presence of God in your life? Let me tell you that is a 100% lie of the enemy who wants to keep you dry and powerless and under his control. It's complete rubbish. On that day in a hot, dusty upper room the Holy Spirit exploded into the lives of every single person waiting there. The only thing they had to do was be obedient to Jesus' command to wait for something to come to them. They weren't perfect either. They would have had flaws and bad attitudes and struggles just like you and me. But when the Holy Spirit came, the only thing that mattered was their hunger.

So lose the self-pity and get hungry for the Holy Spirit. Let me tell you, if you wait around to feel worthy of Him, you'll be waiting until your last days. None of us are worthy, only He is worthy. If He has promised to give us His Holy Spirit why would He pick and choose whom to fill? That's saying that God doesn't keep His promises, which defames His very nature and brings Him down to our level. It's best not to do that.

There's no time like the present, so if you have read these words and you can sense a hunger bubbling up inside for the Holy Spirit to fill you up, pray with me now.

"Holy Spirit, I no longer want to disqualify myself from receiving Your power. Trying to live a good Christian life is all very well, but it isn't enough for me. I need something that will take me to a whole new level of understanding who You are and what is available to me as a citizen of Your kingdom. I'm tired of feeling like I'm outside the camp. I want to partner with you in a life of miracles as You promised I could. So just like You did that day in Acts, and every day since somewhere across the world, will you come and fill me up to overflowing and burn Your passion into my heart for a life of power and authority on earth as it is in heaven. Thank you. Amen."

Expect to see things change from now on.

Enduring strength

I meet so many Christians who tell me they are so tired and weary that they can't carry on. I can be listening to them talk about the reasons why a life with God is exhausting or depressing or restrictive or confusing and have some sympathy, but after ten or fifteen minutes I feel like falling asleep. I don't want to be rude, but Jesus didn't come to give us life in all its fullness only to have us sit and moan about how difficult it is or what a struggle we find it. He didn't give us The Lord's Prayer with the words For Yours is the kingdom and the power only to have us bottle out when things get too exhausting.

I know what it's like to feel tired. I can have weeks where I zig zag up and down the country to minister at different things, come home and then fly off early the next morning to some other country to do a week or more of intense ministry. Sometimes I look at my diary and wonder how on earth I'm physically going to do it all.

How do I manage it? God gives me enduring strength. It's part of the power of God and it's time we believed it when Scripture says,

He gives power to the weak,
And to those who have no might He increases strength.

Even the youths shall faint and be weary,
And the young men shall utterly fall,
But those who wait on the Lord
Shall renew their strength;
They shall mount up with wings like eagles,
They shall run and not be weary,
They shall walk and not faint. Isaiah 40:29-31

God gives us strength so we will always win. It doesn't mean we will always feel light-hearted or victorious, but His strength is more than a feeling. During the times when life saps our energy we have to lay hold of the promise of God that we will rise with a new strength when we wait on Him. His power in us equips us for every season and event of our lives and it's His will and authority that has the last word in every situation. Of course we get tired or weary, but it doesn't need to end there because there is always refreshment and strength available to us in order that we can begin to fly again. So don't live life with your eyes to the ground. Look up and trust Him!

Increased ability

Watching my grandchildren grow up is one of my greatest joys. They change so fast. One time I can be looking after them and they just sit there not doing a lot, but the next time they can be trying to crawl. Soon enough they are walking, then they're running and it's a whole new world because they need watching every minute! With each new thing they learn, I see how frustrated they can get when they're on the brink of a new skill but they haven't quite nailed it.

It's the same with us. As we grow up in our Christian life, we change. We were never supposed to stay the same because the Bible tells us we go from glory to glory.

But we all, with unveiled face, beholding as in a mirror the glory of the Lord, are being transformed into the same image from glory to glory, just as by the Spirit of the Lord. 2 Corinthians 3:18

Each of us has a natural set of talents and gifts embedded in our DNA which are inherited from our family line. Some people are musical, some are good at DIY and some are great problem solvers. One of the things that makes life so interesting is the variety of skills and gifts evident in the people around us and it helps us to need and appreciate one another.

Unless He tells you something different, God will always work with your already established gifts and talents. He knows what makes us tick and He knows what we are good at and what we enjoy. When the Holy Spirit fills us with more and more of His power, we find that we can do more of the things we already do, but with increased ability.

Let me explain what I mean.

I'm not very good when it comes to tinkering under the bonnet of a car. If there's a rattle or knocking sound when I am driving, or if something important has dropped out of the engine, or the battery is dead, it doesn't come naturally to me to fix it. I can try, and sometimes I might succeed, but it's probably better and safer if I get someone else to sort it. It might cost me more, but it's worth it.

But if you ask me to sit down and knock up a sermon in ten minutes, it's as easy as pie. If my secretary comes in wanting ten thoughts for the day before one o'clock, I can do it straight away without really thinking about it.

Why? Because God has given me the ability to do it. It used to be impossible in the old days because I could neither read nor write, but God has helped me to change all that. Yes, I made the effort, but I believe He overlaid it with His Spirit, which has enabled me to do far more than I ever thought possible. If God gives us the power and the authority, He also gives us the ability, and just like my developing grandchildren, we grow in our ability under His watchful care.

If you're a bit timid when it comes to praying for people, it's not because you can't do it, it's because you need to do more of it. Like a child who learns to walk, the more it is practiced, the easier it becomes. Step out in faith, because all power and authority is given to you to achieve more than you could ever think possible.

Dynamic church

There are many wonderful works that are different from miracles. Sometimes I look around the room in my church and my eyes well up as I see faithful servants of God just getting on and serving Him and His body. There's the worship team, the team who administer the food programmes, the family centre guys, the counselors, the prayer ministry team and those who are skilled in working with autism in our autism centre. I look at the stewards, the PA team, the children's workers and I'm just over-the-top thankful for them all. They all do mighty works, equipped by the power and authority of the Holy Spirit and I praise God for each and every one of them.

But as well as such "works" we have been promised a life of miracles. We can't have one without the other. The early church modelled it beautifully with a combination of good organization and governance and mighty works"

And they continued steadfastly in the apostles' doctrine and fellowship, in the breaking of bread, and in prayers. Then fear came upon every soul, and many wonders and signs were done through the apostles. Now all who believed were together, and had all things in common, and sold their possessions and goods, and divided them among all, as anyone had need. So continuing daily with one accord in the temple, and breaking bread from house to house, they ate their food with gladness and simplicity of heart, praising God and having favour with all the people. And the Lord added to the church daily those who were being saved. Acts 2:42-47

In addition to this fantastic relational community there was added amazing miracles, such as the healing of the lame man in Acts 3:1-11.

Church is not the middle-class social action arm of the Almighty and it's not a Sunday version of a golf club. It is the place of radical, powerful encounter with the King of Kings and Lord of Lords, which challenges the heart of man. Church should not take you on an airy-fairy philosophical journey full of waffle, but should lead you into an encounter with the transforming presence of a wonderful God. It is the Holy Spirit who reveals the truth about God through His word so that we are encouraged to live life understanding the consequences of sin, but free from the eternal judgment of it, embracing the freedom of grace.

Church is like a power station. It's a place where the supernatural should be natural and miracles are normal.

We go to church to be topped up and refilled so that when we step into society we can be salt and light, as Peter and John were that day on the way to the Temple.

When church becomes a tea party or a philosophical debating society it loses the power that was promised to it by Jesus and may God have mercy on us for it. What more do we need? God's Word is unequivocal that His kingdom comes through power encounters, when the boundaries of expectation and normal human behaviour are flattened by the work of the Holy Spirit.

There are often times when we can not meet the needs of a person in the natural, so we have to offer them the supernatural.

We have to allow the Holy Spirit to do His work His way. Let's not cork the bottle of His power and authority because of a fear of the unknown. Let's reject the temptation to accept the symptoms of a disease or infirmity and go to the Great Physician for the answer. I'm not against doctors, but they don't have the answer for everything and if we think they do, we are living in deception.

When He was on earth, Jesus was the answer when there was no answer. No one could cure a blind man in the natural, but Jesus spat on mud, smeared it on his eyes and healed him. When a paralytic was lowered through the roof and laid at Jesus' feet in a crowded room, He didn't see anything that was outside of His ability to heal. When a naked man brim full of demons was writhing in front of Him, Jesus' compassion delivered him and then asked for him to be given clothes.

We are delegated servants of the kingdom. What Jesus did, we can do (and more, remember!) by the same power and authority given to us by the power of the Holy Spirit. I am not "David Carr Ministries Inc." I am just David Carr ministering under the authority of the King of Kings. Any power that flows through me in miracles and signs and wonders happens because of Who lives in me.

He has changed me. Will you let Him do the same?

Time to Reflect

You are worthy, O Lord,
To receive glory and honour and power;
For You created all things,
And by Your will they exist and were created.
Revelation 4:11

Think about God for a moment:

- He is worthy of all our praise because He is all the Bible says He is and more
- There is only good in Him
- He has known you even before you were born
- He has watched you grow, day by day, never taking His eyes off you
- He has amazing ideas about how you can partner together for the rest of your life
- He will shape His plans to fit you because you are unique, with a unique personality and set of gifts and talents
- He loves you and never wants you to be afraid of Him or His Holy Spirit because He is a kind Father who would never hurt you or manipulate you
- You are not excluded; you are included.

Meditate

Some people seek to be filled with the Holy Spirit for years and, when it doesn't seem to have happened, they stop talking about it because they are disappointed. Others don't realize that being filled with the Holy Spirit is a daily function not just a one-off experience to get them into the club. Everyone, regardless of their historical church background or specific theological standpoint is eligible to receive power when the Holy Spirit comes upon them. It is then when His authority and power comes that we are enabled to live the life God has destined for us as His children. Put your hand on your heart now and say this prayer with me:

"Father God, I want to thank you that Jesus Christ, Your Son, had the power and the authority to die on a cross to release me from my sin and set me free. I ask you Lord by what you've done for me to accept me just as I am today. I turn away from my self-centred life and I turn to you, expectant that You will change me now. I ask you to forgive me and to wash me clean in the name of Jesus."

"Father God, I want to thank you that because of Pentecost I now have the ability to ask and receive the power to be a witness and I want to receive this dunamis right now. I ask You, Holy Spirit, to fill me afresh and release me to be all that You have called me to be. Use me to spread Your kingdom far and wide for the glory of Your wonderful Name. Amen."

10. Glory

...And the glory...

Years ago I used to sing a hymn which had these words as the chorus:

Turn your eyes upon Jesus,

Look full in His wonderful face,

And the things of earth will grow strangely dim,

In the light of His glory and grace.

We come now to the part of The Lord's Prayer that dwells on God's glory. The sentence about it isn't very long, in fact blink and you'd miss it, but is as important a theme as any in the rest of the prayer.

The word "glory" is so expressive. It is full of weighty meaning such as "splendour, honour, magnificence, copiousness, high renown" and "brilliant, radiant beauty". Time and time again throughout Scripture we read of God's glory being magnificent, abundant, all yielding and never-ending.

When He decides to show His glory, God can do it in any and every part of His creation and into any and every situation.

He may show His glory to an individual:

But You, O Lord are a shield for me, my glory and the One who lifts up my head. Psalm 3:3

Or He may display it across the universe and beyond:

O Lord, our Lord, how excellent is Your name in all the earth, who have set Your glory above the heavens! Psalm 8:1

However it is expressed, God's glory is uncontainable, unfathomable and unexplainable. It exists whether we feel it or not and it is there whether we experience it or not. Jesus encourages His disciples to pray "…and the glory" as a statement of fact, not an optional extra. God is a God of glory and that's that.

What that means for you and me is that we can experience His glory in our finances, our relationships, our workplace, our church, our family, and throughout the whole of our lives, no matter what gets thrown at us. I get so excited about this because it doesn't matter how bleak things become, how at the end of my rope I feel or how confusing life is – my God is still glorious, still magnificent and still radiates with beauty. As the verse above says, He can lift my head so that my eyes are diverted from the things of this earth as I gaze on His glory.

So this one little word explains the magnificence of God and all He represents. I want to look into a passage of Scripture that will help us understand it a bit more.

The promise of God's presence

Then Moses said to the Lord, 'See, You say to me, "Bring up this people." But You have not let me know whom You will send with me. Yet You have said, 'I know you by name, and you have also found grace in My sight.' Now therefore, I pray, if I have found grace in Your sight, show me now Your way, that I may know You and that I may find grace in Your sight. And consider that this nation is Your people."

And He said, 'My Presence will go with you, and I will give you rest.' Then he said to Him, 'If Your Presence does not go with us; do not bring us up from here. For how then will it be known that Your people and I have found grace in Your sight, except You go with us? So we shall be separate, Your people and I, from all the people who are upon the face of the earth.' So the Lord said to Moses, 'I will also do this thing that you have spoken; for you have found grace in My sight, and I know you by name.' And he said, 'Please, show me Your glory.' Then He said, 'I will make all My goodness pass before you, and I will proclaim the name of the Lord before you. I will be gracious to whom I will be gracious, and I will have compassion on whom I will have compassion.' But He said, 'You cannot see My face; for no man shall see Me, and live.' And the Lord said, 'Here is a place by Me, and you shall stand on the rock. So it shall be, while My glory passes by, that I will put you in the cleft of the rock, and will cover you with My hand while I pass by. Then I will take away My hand, and you shall see My back; but My face shall not be seen.' Exodus 33:12-23

What a graphic story this is. At the heart of the interaction between Moses and God is the cry of Moses to know God's presence and that God would show him the way. In one sense, Moses is expressing a desire to know Jesus, who was to say of Himself many centuries later,

I am the way, the truth, and the life. No one comes to the Father except through Me. John 14:6

Even in the Old Testament people were still looking for the Saviour. Just because He hadn't been born in the days before Mary and Joseph, it didn't mean He didn't exist. Jesus has always existed and has always been in relationship with His Father and the Holy Spirit, way before He was a little baby in a manger. In Genesis chapter one, when God is about to create man, He says,

Then God said, 'Let Us make man in Our image, according to Our likeness...' Genesis 1:26

The "Us" here denotes the unity within the Trinity: Father, Son and Holy Spirit. Man will therefore be created to reflect the image of all three, including Jesus.

So even though Moses would never have known Jesus, he was still looking for the Way. In the following verses, God answers Moses by showing him some of the aspects of His glory, which will only be revealed to him if he remains hidden in the rock. God will pass by in His glory, but Moses will only be allowed to see the back of God, not His face, such is the brilliance of it.

This lucid conversation between Moses and God happened at a time of great change. The children of Israel had been up to all sorts of ungodly things including fashioning and then worshipping a calf of gold while Moses was up on Mount Sinai in a glory cloud receiving the Law, including the Ten Commandments which he wrote on tablets of stone. On his descent, Moses was appalled by the behaviour of the people and in a holy rage he smashed the stone tablets in front of them.

It is from this place of desperation, disappointment and anger that Moses learns a fresh hunger for the glory of God. He wants nothing more of this impurity and filth and as leader of the children of Israel his cry to God is please show me Your glory! He knows he can't lead the people without it and he knows the people won't follow without it.

If the filth and perversion of this world doesn't drive you into the purity of God, you can't do anything but remain in a mess. If God's glory doesn't come down into our lives and change our perspective, we stay tainted by the idolatry and impurity around us. Moses didn't want that and I don't want that, do you?

But before Moses even asked God to show him His glory, there were seven steps he needed to take in order to prepare himself to receive it.

Preparing for glory

- *He didn't want to go on his own.* Moses may have been a strong and capable leader with all kinds of gifts for the job, but he knew there was no point leading anyone or anything on his own. He craved the companionship of God. This is a good one to remember. In all our grand schemes we may have to change the world for God, or if we're a leader, lead our people into amazing exploits in His Name. But we are lost without His presence. Don't go it alone; no one will thank you for it in the end and it will just exhaust you.

- *He knew God knew his name.* Moses tells God that he knows him by name and that God has given him divine favour and grace. He hasn't got an identity crisis and he's not indulging in false humility either, because he is confident in his standing as God's man for the job. How often we can think that we have to tell God again and again what's going on with us as if He didn't know. He knows us all by name and we are His beloved children! When we ask for His glory we don't have to simper about it, we can approach Him with boldness and confidence.

- *He looks for the way.* It wasn't enough for Moses to float around and just "go with the flow". He knew God had a plan and he wanted to know what it was. He asked God to show him the way, which acknowledged God as the ultimate leader. When did you last stop to ask God to show you the way? You might be surprised by the plans He is waiting to share with you.

- *He knew who was really in charge.* Moses came to God on behalf of the people. At no stage did he try to upstage God or get protective about his role as leader. Israel belonged to God and Moses saw his role as steward of the people, not owner of the people. The original call to lead them from slavery in Egypt and into the desert came directly from God because He cared about His people. If we are to see more of the glory of God revealed to us, we need to lose our grip on the visions or people we think belong to us and release them back to the Lord. The churches I lead are not mine, they are God's and He's in charge, so what He says goes.

- *He knew God's presence was there.* After Moses had stood in a glory cloud on Mount Sinai, he was in no doubt that the presence of God was real. God has promised us that He will never leave us or forsake us. We are not left to amble aimlessly around life until we finally die and do to heaven. God's presence is in us and all around us, every day and every night, so the visitation of His glory is in some ways an extension of what is already there – just more intense!

- *He refuses to go anywhere without it.* Moses pleaded with God to send His presence and keep it there. He knew that there was no point embarking on a journey into anything unless they were surrounded by it. How often can we get all excited about a new vision or job or relationship and forget to invite the presence of God to walk with us in it? By refusing to walk without Him, we invite more grace, more power, more love, more revelation and more glory into what would otherwise become a cold and lonely road.

- *He knew it would set them apart.* After the Israelites had lived in slavery in Egypt at the beck and call of a foreign ruler, Moses was ready to lead a people with their own identity. As the people of God, Israel would stand separate from any other nation around it, which would require God to stamp His unique mark on it. Not just the Law, but the Spirit: the Presence. If we want to live in the glory of God we must understand that we will be in the world but not of it. We can be relevant to our society without indulging in the sinful behaviours of it. Like Jesus, we are to be friends of sinners but not allow the sin itself to contaminate our flesh.

So it was only after this sevenfold journey that Moses then asked God the question "Please show me Your glory." In the same way, we can't just ask God to turn up like a magician with bells and whistles to impress people. His glory is holy and He is King and Lord. Don't mess with Him. Get yourself ready to receive Him as Moses did.

Some people aren't ready to do all that preparation stuff, and I'm sorry if this sounds harsh, but if that is the case, they will never know the fullness of God.

In my own walk with God, I am careful to take all those seven points above very seriously indeed in my journey towards more of His glory being revealed in my life and the lives of those around me. But I honestly wouldn't have it any other way.

People sometimes come up to me and say, "Pastor Dave, I don't know how you do it. You've been in ministry for forty years now and you seem to have as much energy now as you did years ago!" I answer them along the lines of, "I'm no more energetic than you, I'm not cleverer than you and I'm certainly not better looking than you. But I know how to obey the seven principles of preparing myself for the glory of God to come."

Some days, I find it hard to leap out of bed because my bones lock and I have to be careful. But by the time I'm at church I can dance around with all the energy of the Lord because I'm standing in the wealth of His presence. It's never a performance for me, it's the anointing of the Holy Spirit that makes me want to dance and shout and sing praises to my God. If I haven't got these seven principles working, I would probably be sitting in a chair groaning and feeling as old as the hills! With my God, I really can run through a troop and leap over a wall!

Receiving the glory

In response to Moses' preparation, God offers eight things in return:

- *Goodness.* God tells Moses that His goodness will pass before Him. In Psalm 23, David writes, "Surely goodness and mercy shall follow me all the days of my life" (Psalm 23:6) and man, don't we need some of that! I'm fed up of everything being bad, aren't you? I want good news and more of it! Goodness will only follow those who acknowledge the principles of God and for those who don't, you find that generally, things don't go that well. It doesn't mean that life is always easy for us, but it does mean that we come under His goodness whatever life may bring.

- *Proclamation.* When God proclaims His name, doors open, people are healed, jobs are given, neighbours stop giving us trouble and the prodigals return. The Lord would proclaim His name before Moses and miracles would happen amongst the people. That just goes with His glorious Name.

- *Favour.* God says to Moses that He will show grace to those He wants to. In other words, God can have favourites! He favours people who worship Him so please don't be offended by that. In our culture we like everyone to be treated the same and we get edgy when we hear preachers talk about rewards or favour. Get used to it! God may not be into favouritism but He does have favourites. Israel was a favoured nation and if you are walking in His kingdom you are one of His favourites, so you had better start wanting to become one His friends! He's worth it, believe me.

- *Compassion*. The dictionary defines compassion as a feeling of distress or pity for those who are suffering and a desire to alleviate it. God tells Moses He will have compassion on His people so they can be free to rest in the assurance of His care. The same is true for us.

- *Hiddenness*. When God removed His face from His people in this instance, it was not out of anger or pain, but because of His power. However, it didn't mean He was remote, so when God had passed by He would lift His hand away from Moses so he could see the back of Him. Let's not be glib about the glory of God, it is immensely powerful and in this passage in Scripture could kill a man if he caught sight of God's face. God hides from us not to withhold His goodness and His glory, but to protect us from the full power of it.

- *Protection*. The rock was there in preparation for such a time when Moses needed to be kept safe. There are times in our lives when we will need to know that God has a safe place ready and waiting for us to hide in. We may not always need it, but it is there nonetheless.

- *Covering*. When Moses did need it, God placed him there. So too, our lives are hidden in Christ, the Rock.

- *Uncovering*. At just the right time, God takes His hand away and Moses can see the glory of His presence. It is God's choice to do this and He does it at just the right time. Remember that God knows what we need before we ask Him, so He will reveal Himself to us in the ways we need it most, at the most appropriate time.

Yours, O Lord is the greatness,
The power and the glory,
The victory and the majesty;
For all that is in heaven and in earth is Yours;
Yours is the kingdom, O Lord,
And You are exalted as head over all. 1 Chronicles 29:11

Hallelujah! Thank You Lord!

Living in the glory

If God turned up with the expanse of His glory today, we would fall on our faces and be paralyzed on the floor because the weight of it would lie heavily on us. I have been in meetings where as a congregation we couldn't stand under the intense weight of His glory. You know when He's there like that; there's no pretending.

When the wealth of His glory fills the heart, there will be an increase in the abundance of the human harvest. In other words, when His glory rests on you, everything you put your hand to increases in success and favour.

Scripture tells us we are going from glory to glory with unveiled faces so we reflect His beauty as we praise and worship Him. Have you ever seen a person's face change to reflect the beauty of God? I have. It's magnificent, I can tell you; like a little foretaste of heaven. His presence brings transformation to our bodies, minds, souls and spirits and His glory is the fullness of joy. Not only that but it transforms the places on which our feet tread. Do you want to change your community for Jesus? The let His glory transform you so you shine with His righteousness and radiance.

Time to Reflect

- Have you spent too long thinking about how to make the latest ideas or projects impact your church and community?
- Do you find yourself getting easily distracted by men's ideas when what you really want is His glory?
- Have you ever prayed for His glory to come without fully surrendering yourself to Him, as Moses did?

Meditate

It's time to reject religion and choose His presence! Look for the glory of God. It won't take you long to find it; He is right beside you now as you read this. His glory will help you if you need more courage. It will help you if you need healing. It will transform your view of the world and His love for it. Lift your eyes and pray with me.

"Lord God, I come to you now weary of my own plans to make things work. I have tried my best to do the right thing. Sometimes I've done okay, but other times I've made a mess. What I need, what I really need, is an encounter with Your presence that will change me forever. I know You are good and I know You are powerful and I know more than even before how much I need You to walk my journey through life with me. I need a hand to hold and I want it to be Yours. I'm not prepared to carry on unless You meet me today. So come Holy Spirit and cover me with Your glory. And then, make me SHINE! Thank you so much. Amen."

11. Eternity

For ever and even

If only we could grasp a deeper understanding of eternity, I believe it would change who we are and how we live our lives. In fact, it's not just a fresh revelation of eternity that would change us, but a fresh revelation of anything at all to challenge our established belief systems. My great concern, when we look at Christendom, is that we have a set of beliefs but they have become passive and entrenched in our traditions and rituals. They prevent us from seeking and finding new understanding in order to grow in the Christian faith.

Active belief actually changes who we are. It may come from a good source or a bad source, but when new ideologies are embraced and allowed to take root, passive faith is replaced with action. Sadly, we have all too often seen the devastating effects of zealous extremism in our nation and in many others across the world in recent times.

As Christians, we should be crying out for the Holy Spirit to come and reveal more truth to us, as Jesus promised He would in the gospel of John:

However, when He, the Spirit of truth, has come, He will guide you into all truth; for He will not speak on His own authority, but whatever He hears He will speak; and He will tell you things to come. John 16:13

If we are full of the Holy Spirit, our belief will be active and not passive and there will be no room for a laid back or lazy attitude. When Jesus comes to the end of The Lord's Prayer, He includes these four simple words, "for ever and ever" as a statement that the kingdom of God will never pass away. It is always present, has always been present and always will be present. God is not going to pack His bags at some point in the future and decide to retire: He is for ever and ever!

Learn to shout out

We are meant to shout out for His kingdom to come and break into our present and into our future. We should be forever grateful for the past testimonies of God's faithfulness to us, of course, but let's not live on those experiences only: let's experience new ones every day and for the rest of our lives!

Look at what happens when a cry goes out to the One whose kingdom breaks in"

Then it happened, as He was coming near Jericho, that a certain blind man sat by the road begging. And hearing a multitude passing by, he asked what it meant. So they told him that Jesus of Nazareth was passing by. And he cried out, saying, 'Jesus, Son of David, have mercy on me!' Then those who went before warned him that he should be quiet; but he cried out all the more, 'Son of David, have mercy on me!' So Jesus stood still and commanded him to be brought to Him. And when he had come near, He asked

him, saying, 'What do you want Me to do for you?' He said, 'Lord,
that I may receive my sight.' Then Jesus said to him, 'Receive your
sight; your faith has made you well.' And immediately he received
his sight, and followed Him, glorifying God. And all the people,
when they saw it, gave praise to God. Luke 18:35-43

There was nothing passive about this blind man. He didn't care who heard his loud cries over and over again. Something inside the beggar woke up to the possibility that Jesus of Nazareth could change his circumstances forever and he wasn't about to be shut up or shut down. His reward was an encounter with this eternal kingdom of God, which came and swept through, not only his physical eyes, but also the eyes of his soul so that he joined the crowd that followed Him with a heart full of praise.

How easy it is to slip into a life of orthodoxy and forget to shout out, "Jesus, Son of David have mercy on me!" as the blind beggar did. It concerns me deeply that we have settled for what we have grown used to as a church and we have lost the power we were promised because we don't want it badly enough. We moan about how we want our lives to be more dynamic; we lament the loss of miracles; we weep when we lose those close to us who die before their time; and we rely on our leaders to keep us entertained when we need it and soothe us when we need it.

My role as church pastor is not to pacify my flock, it's to stir them into a life with God that gets progressively more exciting, deep and miraculous. I'm not here to entertain people and I'm not here to laud it over people either. If people don't like my preaching style, I don't care to be honest. I simply want to lead them to a place where they can meet the One who is forever and ever and who can and will transform any situation they may be facing into one that has His kingdom all over it.

Learn to cry out

How lovely is Your tabernacle, O Lord of hosts! My soul longs, yes, even faints for the courts of the Lord; my heart and my flesh cry out for the living God. Psalm 84:1-2

The whole quest of man is for eternity and to know that there is a sustainability of life. Why else do we go to the doctors? We want to live because we appreciate life. I remember once how I prayed for a lady in Singapore who had been unconscious for four years. Her husband, a hospital consultant asked me to pray for a miracle for his pediatrician wife to wake up. It had cost £2 million to keep her alive. Their children would go there and cry over her and the situation the family found themselves in. They were crying out for a miracle, which we did not see in an earthly sense, but who knows what happened in the eternal realm?

If the only thing on which we base our lives is the "here and now" then all we ever become is disappointed and hard-hearted. When we let our flesh and our heart cry out to the living God, it goes beyond our need for life as we know it and takes us into eternity. The lady in the coma may not have been restored in this life, but she belonged to God and ultimately, His care for her was not restricted by her current physical state at the time.

Yes, our shouts and cries should be for His kingdom to come and His will to be done in our present reality on earth as it is in heaven, but they should also echo into eternity which is outside of time altogether and where everything is beautiful. Time is an invasion into eternity: it is unnatural and was never initially part of the plan for creation. Time itself was a consequence of the rebellion in the Garden of Eden, which changed everything and was only redeemed on the Cross.

Solomon nails it

In the book of Ecclesiastes there is a statement written by Solomon that could easily go unnoticed in amongst all the other stuff. What he wrote in a few short words is so profound that it never fails to blow me away when I read it or when I preach on it. It says,

He has made everything beautiful in its time. Also He has put eternity in their hearts, except that no one can find out the work that God does from beginning to end. Ecclesiastes 3:11

There is a difference between "for ever and ever" and "eternity". When Jesus told His disciples to pray for ever and ever, He was talking about what is to come. It is a futuristic phrase, if you like, in the same way that if I say I will love you for ever and ever I am saying that I will love you from this point on into the future. "Ever and ever" doesn't refer to the past at all, which makes it very different from the meaning of "eternity".

When Solomon writes that God has set eternity into the hearts of men, He is saying that no one can find out the work that God does from beginning to end because God has no beginning! Eternity is about the past, the present and the future, all rolled into one and all outside our understanding of the concept of time. Human beings live within the confines of time and motion, but God doesn't. He is eternal and He had no beginning and will have no end. We find that an impossible concept to grasp hold of because since the Fall, we were not able to think in those ways. The most brilliant scientists and philosophers can grapple for a lifetime trying to get their heads around it all, but in the end even they have to admit defeat.

God sits outside of our capabilities of understanding and yet it has not stopped Him setting eternity in our hearts. Just because we don't understand it doesn't mean it's not true!

The breath of God

God is the only Being who is immortal. At the point of the creation of man, everything was perfect and nothing could spoil it. Adam and then Eve were in perfect relationship with God and nature, in a place where there was no sin or death. Although man was created and immortal, unlike God, he did have a beginning so was not eternal. But knowing that His intention is that this man will have His nature within him, God breathes His eternity into him

And the Lord God formed man of the dust of the ground, and breathed into his nostrils the breath of life; and man became a living being. Genesis 2:7

Writing in Ecclesiastes, Solomon understands how God has put an eternal spirit into man which nobody can fully understand, because whilst his flesh has a beginning and an end, the breath of God within does not. Unless a person acknowledges this eternal part of his or her life as alive in Christ, the Bible tells us they are dead and will spend eternity separated from its original source. This is the part of man designed to live outside of the physical body and is what makes us who we are, freeing us into a destiny with God for eternity.

For thus says the High and Lofty One
Who inhabits eternity, whose name is Holy:
'I dwell in the high and holy place,
With him who has a contrite and humble spirit,
To revive the spirit of the humble,
And to revive the heart of the contrite ones.' Isaiah 57:15

As far back as Genesis we see the eternal God giving promises that will last forever. It is as if His breath has been breathed out into His creation since time began and will continue until all comes to an end.

The rainbow promise

The covenant made between God and Noah in Genesis was not a temporary one, but an everlasting one.

And God said: 'This is the sign of the covenant which I make between Me and you, and every living creature that is with you, for perpetual generations: I set My rainbow in the cloud, and it shall be for the sign of the covenant between Me and the earth. It shall be, when I bring a cloud over the earth, that the rainbow shall be seen in the cloud; and I will remember My covenant which is between Me and you and every living creature of all flesh; the waters shall never again become a flood to destroy all flesh. The rainbow shall be in the cloud, and I will look on it to remember the everlasting covenant between God and every living creature of all flesh that is on the earth.' Genesis 9:12-16

When God makes a promise He will never change His mind. Here He promises Noah that there will never again be a flood on the same scale as there was then, with such devastating consequences. When He speaks of "never again" in the passage above, He means just that, never again. This everlasting covenant is set from that point on until the end of time and nothing will ever revoke it.

The pregnancy promise

The covenant between God and Abram in Genesis chapter 12 is one of the most important in the whole of Scripture. The call of God comes to him to leave his land and take his wife Sarai and his family and all his possessions and travel to a new land.

Now the Lord had said to Abram: 'Get out of your country, from your family and from your father's house, to a land that I will show you. I will make you a great nation; I will bless you and make your name great; and you shall be a blessing. I will bless those who bless you, and I will curse him who curses you; and in you all the families of the earth shall be blessed.' Genesis 12:1-3

Abram does just that and, in the process, not only does God change his name to Abraham and his wife's name to Sarah, but God breathes His eternal promise of a child to this old man and his barren wife, which fulfilled the promise made to him that he would be a father to many nations on the earth. Through his descendants, Abraham's name would always be "Father of many".

It was the implanting of the eternal that transformed this couple's internal and external lives forever when Isaac was born.

How David writes about it

But the mercy of the Lord is from everlasting to everlasting on those who fear Him. Psalm 103:17

When he wrote the Psalms King David had to explain the eternal nature of God in some way or another and he chose to do it by using the phrase, from everlasting to everlasting, which on the surface is a contradiction in terms. If you are everlasting, there is nowhere you can go to, especially not from everlasting to everlasting! But in writing it this way, David is going a long way to explaining that God has always been and will always be. In other words, God is not just projecting forwards into the future, but backwards into the past. His eternal nature means that there has never been a time when God did not exist and there will never be a time when he ceases to be. He is a permanent fixture, a constant presence yesterday, today and tomorrow.

David would never see Jesus in the flesh, but from his writings in the Psalms he knew that God was sending His presence into the world at some point in some way. He also knew that God was his salvation, his saviour whom he could trust for the whole of his life.

The Lord is my light and my salvation; whom shall I fear? Psalm 27:1

David knew his destiny was to spend eternity with God when he died and his life was lived in preparation for it.

Our eternal home

We never know when our time on earth is up. For that reason, we need to really deeply consider where we will go when we die. Where will your eternal home be? I know where I will be because I know to whom my life belongs and I know He has prepared a place for me to live in when I do eventually die.

In Matthew 25, Jesus speaks about the everlasting fire that is prepared for the devil and his angels and the everlasting punishment reserved for those who spend their lives rejecting God. We don't just float off into nowhere when we die! We all have a destiny and we need to consider whether our for ever and ever is in heaven or whether it is in hell. I don't want to scare you on this, but neither will I avoid it. John's gospel tells us that God loved the world so much He sent His one and only Son to die for it, so that those who will believe in Him will not perish but have everlasting life (John 3:16). Jesus came to give us life in all its fullness, not just so we could live as human beings for a few short years enjoying the benefits, but so that the eternity that has been already set in our hearts can also be our reality in the afterlife. What we currently know is not all there is. He is for ever and ever and He is eternal and everlasting. Why would it all end when we die? His forgiveness is everlasting, His love is everlasting and His mercy is everlasting. Hallelujah!

When we receive Jesus into our lives, from that moment on we are secured into an eternal home for ever and ever. In other words, the everlasting starts from that moment on.

Life can suddenly change

A good few years ago I was asked to help out a footballer who was coming to the end of his career with Oxford United. After his accountant made a few terrible decisions, Peter was left destitute and my job was to help him sort it all out. He was a lovely man with a fabulous wife, Sally, and they had two children aged six and four at the time.

I told him that as he was financially at the end of his rope after being ripped off so badly, he should move into a little bungalow he owned in Wantage with his family and start building himself up again bit-by-bit. I remember going to see him on a Friday and telling him I would get him the cheapest insurance policy I could possibly find to save him as much as possible while he tried to get back on his feet. I sat there with Peter and Sally that day as they signed the forms and when I left, I said a cheery goodbye, assuring them I would submit the documents on Monday and it would all be sorted.

That Sunday I went to church as usual and Molly left early to get the dinner ready for the children. When I walked back into the house, her face was as white as a sheet. She asked me if I had seen Peter and Sally on the Friday and I told her I had, and she went on to tell me that she had just heard on the news that they were both dead. Apparently they had just left their friend's house after having a meal together when a drunk driver hit them as he came over the hill.

I couldn't believe it. Only two days previously I had been sitting with them planning their future and getting as good a deal as I could to help them recover financially. In fact I still had their application forms in my briefcase.

On the Monday morning I went to the insurance company and explained the situation and to cut a long story short, I was able to secure the full amount without any premium, which meant their two small children were provided for until they came of age as the money was able to buy a beautiful house for them to grow up in and they were cared for there by Peter's sister.

Do you see how life can change, just like that? In a split second, all the plans and ideas we had talked about for this family's life were wiped out and two children were left parentless.

God never changes

The only One who never changes is our Father in Heaven. Whatever life throws at us and whatever situation we find ourselves in, nothing is outside of God's ability to draw us deeper into His eternal, everlasting love and protection.

Remember what Paul writes to the church in Corinth?

For this corruptible must put on incorruption, and this mortal must put on immortality. 1 Corinthians 15:53

To put on immortality is to invite the everlasting, eternal breath of God by His Holy Spirit to breathe into our own spirit, sparking it into life for ever. In Jesus, we are incorruptible because we carry the same Spirit who raised Christ from the dead. That means that death really is swallowed up in victory and our eternal destiny is secure. Whilst our mortal bodies deteriorate and eventually die, our immortal lives are being transformed daily by the eternal promise and timeless energy of God.

For God so loved the world that He gave His only begotten Son, that whoever believes in Him should not perish but have everlasting life. John 3:16

Time to Reflect

Is there anxiety and uncertainty in your heart today? If life should deal you a cruel blow, do you have the assurance of eternal life with God? Let me encourage you to open your heart to the peace of God, which is beyond any understanding you may currently have, or any anxiety that has gripped hold of you. He is our Father. We are encouraged to approach Him as children at any time, for anything, no matter how long we have been a Christian or even if we are not yet a Christian. He prefers it when we are honest with Him about our fears because then He can turn them into joy.

Let me just say that if you have not yet repented and given your heart to Jesus, there is no time like the present! At the end of this chapter is a short, simple prayer you can pray to invite Jesus to come and change you and set you free. Make sure you tell someone you have done it and then get stuck into a church!

Let Him lead you as we pray together now.

Meditate

"Lord God, you are the eternal and everlasting King. You were not created by anyone or anything. You have always existed and will never cease to exist and You aren't confined to my way of thinking or living. I know that one day my life on earth will end and I am conscious of my eternal destiny right now. I want You to lead me into a fresh assurance of hope that I will spend eternity with You because I can't imagine eternity being separated from You. Free me from all my fears and fill me with joy, eternal Father, everlasting God. Thank you. Amen."

A prayer of repentance

"Lord, I choose to give my life to You today. I repent of all my sin and turn away from a life that has been lived without You in it. Please forgive me and come and set me free so that I can learn to walk with You in the fullness of life that You have promised for me. I want to change and I want to give You the permission to clean me out from deep inside so that I become more and more like You every day. Thank you. Amen."

12. Amen

...Amen.

So we come now to the final part of this wonderful prayer. The word "amen" may be small, and considered by some to be an afterthought at the end of a prayer, but in biblical terms it is extremely significant. When Jesus told His disciples to pray in this way, He did not use the final "amen" as religious glue to seal the prayer together, He used it to indicate that everything He had declared in the previous words was exactly what He said it was. It was as if He was saying all I have said is everything you need and the truths I have spoken out are not just true now, but will be true always.

I have heard the word "amen" used in so many different ways over the years. In extreme situations it has been said to assert the views of graceless people who think their opinions are held by God in heaven and the amen is just agreeing with them. For instance, a preacher may say that because of some misdemeanour the person who committed it is going to hell. When he asks for an amen, the congregation readily responds "amen" relegating the word to a form of fleshly agreement with the views of their leader. It is not the correct use for the word and makes me want to say, "Excuse me, do you know what you are saying?"

This little word shouldn't be used as a religious platitude or a ritual habit to end a prayer neatly. It is there to assert that what has gone before is true and is exactly as it should be. For the disciples it was true and it remains true for each and every one of us today.

It may be small, but it carries infinite weight and authority!

What are we saying amen to?

Over the previous twelve chapters we have examined the key themes of this beautiful prayer and my hope is that along our journey you have received a fresh revelation of Jesus. If all we were to do in this chapter was to package it all up and amen it, putting it on a shelf where it will remain as a nice little book with some good ideas, it would defeat the whole object of me writing it in the first place!

You see, the amen requires our engagement and response. Let me remind you what we are saying amen to:

- We say amen to God being our Father. Not a Father, not even the Father, but my Father. From the very start, the truth is clear that this prayer is rooted in a personal relationship with the Almighty as we are bonded in to the Giver of life who invites us to sit on His lap and who puts His arms around us. As a young boy I would love Sunday nights since it was the night when my Mum would go to church and my Dad would sit listening to the radio in his chair, wearing his coat as we would have no heating on in the house. Dad would let me sit on his lap and I would rest my head near his heart and I would feel safe from the terrors of the dark. When it was time for bed, he would pick me up with his old gnarled hands that smelled of leather from his workshop, put me on his shoulders and give me a piggyback up what he called "the old wooden hill". He was so patient with me and so when I pray "Our Father" I know what it means. There are good fathers and bad fathers, kind fathers and indifferent fathers, but whatever our own experience, our Heavenly Abba (Daddy) is nothing but good.

- We say amen to the rule of Heaven. There will never be any other God like ours, who came down from Heaven and embraced the whole human experience from beginning to end. Jesus knows what it feels like to be human because He became one. Read what the writer of John's Gospel says: "And the Word became flesh and dwelt among us, and we beheld His glory, the glory as of the only begotten of the Father, full of grace and truth" (John 1:14). Whilst we must never undervalue the importance of Jesus' earthly ministry, it is not on earth where God's rule and reign is based; He rules from Heaven. All of His governance and rule takes place outside of our earthly restrictions and expectations. In Heaven there is no sickness, no disease, no pain, no sorrow and no conflict, but only peace, joy, health and wholeness. There He sits on His throne as King of Kings and Lord of Lords and nothing has ever, can ever or will ever change that. God is in Heaven and so we say "amen" to it!

- We say amen to the holiness of His Name. In chapter three we learned more about how God's name expresses His nature and character. His Name is not simply a label to pin on Him in a crowded room full of different gods in order to identify Him as a particular Deity. No! He is the God: the one and only Lord. Throughout the ages, His Name has been revered and respected and honoured as infinitely holy, ultimately powerful and achingly loving. The acknowledgement of it right at the start of The Lord's Prayer, coming just after His identity as Father, leaves no room for any other gods to get a look in. Hallelujah!

- We say amen to a different kind of Kingdom. While the kingdom rule of God is seated in heavenly places, we are given free access to the benefits of it while we live on earth. Jesus told His disciples to pray, "Your Kingdom come," making it very clear that God is not a selfish old man peering at His creation from far away, letting it struggle on with earthly governance and man's vain plans and ambitions. Remember, He is the God of the impossible, in whose Kingdom all manner of wonderful and miraculous things are completely normal. Healing, provision, blessing, manifestations of glory and so on are all possible here on earth when we make room for His presence. It makes me want to shout my "amen", not whisper it!

- We say amen to His perfect will for our lives. Obedience to God's will doesn't mean we relinquish our own will to become silly robots that can't think or act for themselves. If we believe that, as His children, God both understands us inside out and also wants the very best for our lives, it shouldn't be a problem to pray "your will be done." God isn't a dictator who barks out orders, making His people anxious and afraid. He is a strong and loving Father who knows how to give good gifts to His children (Matthew 7:11). Not only that, but His is very much in the business of making people's circumstances change for the better. In other words, we see from the ministry of Jesus how some terrible situations were changed for the better in an instant as the lame were healed, the demon possessed were set free and the dead were raised to life again. So if it is, as the Bible says it is, God's will to make all things new and give people life in all it's fullness, that has to deserve a resounding amen!

- We say amen to His ability to look after us. Do you remember how God looked after His people Israel while they were wandering in the desert? Every day He would faithfully provide food, or manna, for them so they didn't go hungry. Sometimes we get anxious about our lack of resources and give way to fear that somehow everything will go pear shaped and we doubt that God either knows what we are going through or that He is even listening to our cries for help. Let me tell you: God knows and God listens. And it doesn't stop there. He has every available resource ready to be used to provide for what we need. God isn't passive or inconsistent. He doesn't decide to provide for some people and not others. One of His names is Jehovah Jireh, my God will provide, and because His Names reflect His character, providing for His children is not something He finds difficult to do. So at the end of this prayer, when you say "amen" you are saying amen to a heaven-full of resources and blessing for you, your loved ones and those you pray for. He is so good! Amen?

- We say amen to His total forgiveness for our sin. One of the very best things about becoming a Christian is the encounter with a God who wipes our slate totally clean. No matter what wrong things we have done, said or thought, the death and resurrection of Jesus means we are no longer condemned by the sin that held us tightly in chains. He has cut those chains forever and when we accept Him as Lord, He sets to work by His Spirit changing us from the inside out from glory to glory. Hallelujah! I get things wrong all the time, but I know that He has forgiven me. With that deep assurance I can then say amen to the power at work in me that helps me to forgive others the wrong they have done against me. For the Christian, forgiveness is not an add-on or an optional extra. Jesus was very clear that we should forgive others just as our Heavenly Father has forgiven us, which isn't always easy, but is never impossible with His help.

- We say amen to staying away from what tempts us. There is no magic on-off switch when it comes to temptation. Just because we are following Jesus we are not exempt from the whisperings of the enemy who tries to coax us into sin. We will keep being tempted as long as we live and not everyone's weaknesses are the same. We need to recognise what our own are, stop flirting on the edge of them, and regularly be honest before God in prayer. We need His help and the help of friends we can trust to be strong and resist temptation. Jesus was in the desert when He passed each of the three tests thrown at Him by the devil who wanted to overpower Him. How we handle temptation will make us either a victim or a victor. In The Lord's Prayer, the cry is don't lead us into it in the first place but if we do find ourselves with a battle to fight, we can be 100% sure we are on the winning side. Let me hear an amen to that.

- We say amen to letting God bail us out. I know the language is different, but deliver us from evil really means the same as get me out of here! Our battle is not against flesh and blood but against the principalities and powers in a world we can't see with our natural eyes. Just because we can't see it doesn't mean it doesn't exist and God does not want us to dabble in darkness. We are commanded to walk in the light as He is in the light: "But if we walk in the light as He is in the light, we have fellowship with one another, and the blood of Jesus Christ His Son cleanses us from all sin" (1 John 1:7). We just need to get on and do it. Walk the walk, not just talk the talk, as they say. For the times it feels impossible to us, and for the times we feel weak and need help, He has promised He will carry us and secure our feet on the path through life. Thank you, my Father.

- We say amen to the fact that it is not our kingdom, but His. The sooner we get this the better. In myself I have no heavenly kingdom authority or power until the Holy Spirit makes His home in my life. If I spend my life idle or full of my own sense of importance, it's very difficult for the values of His kingdom to flow through me. What are these values? They are manifested as the fruits and gifts of the Spirit that Paul writes about in his letters to the churches in Corinth and Galatia and include love, joy, goodness, self-control, the gift of tongues, prophecy and healing. Evidence of these qualities is the evidence of His kingdom. Are we engaging in that power today? Shouldn't we be seeking them as Paul says and praying for more of His kingdom to come and reign in our lives? Yes and amen.

- We say amen to the manifestation of His glory all around the world. God's glory is excessive, lavish, splendid and magnificent. It is the majestic aura of His holiness and when it descends from heaven, it is impossible to ignore. Many are unable to stand under the sheer weight and beauty of it. The reality is that we see far less of it than we should or could because we keep our eyes focussed on the task in hand which is week by week church meetings or serving the poor, doing soup runs and so on. All these things are wonderful in their place and we shouldn't stop doing them. But there is more! More glory, more wonder, more power, more beauty, more of everything heaven has to offer. If we could only lead people to the place of His glory and His presence who didn't know Him, they would encounter something so amazing it would take their breath away. We can evangelize people for years and years and nothing happens. Give them a glory encounter with the King of Kings and hearts are changed forever in an instant. Come Lord and send more of Your glory. Amen.

- We say amen to His eternal existence. God has set eternity in every human heart. Every person alive has the potential to host the nature and character of the God who made them. It's not a small thing, it's huge. God is for ever and ever and by depositing some of that "ever and ever" within humanity He invests a part of Himself in us. It's a sobering thought and one which should cause us to fall on our knees in humility at the enormous privilege of it. When man's mortality one day gets swallowed up and changed to immortality, our future is eternally assured. In other words, we will live with God forever. For now, while we live on earth, we have a deposit of the promise ahead, not yet realised in its fullness but still of immense value. When we say amen to the "for ever and ever" we are standing in the truth that all we see now is not all there is to come. Our lives on earth are short in comparison to the lives we have ahead of us in Christ. In thanking God for our own salvation and future destiny, let's remember those we know whose eternal destiny in Christ is not yet secure and pray for them to come to a full knowledge of Him.

He's coming back

He who testifies to these things says, 'Surely I am coming quickly.' Amen. Even so, come, Lord Jesus! The grace of our Lord Jesus Christ be with you all. Amen. Revelation 22:20-21

John wrote these words as an indication of what was to come. God is always on the move one way or another, changing circumstances for the better, transforming bodies, minds and spirits with one touch. Throughout history, people have testified to the way the Holy Spirit suddenly turns up and changes everything.

One day, a time will come when Jesus returns and everything is made new. If we know God, we will be raised to life again just as Jesus was on the third day at His resurrection.

As we draw this book to a close, I want you to remember that this remarkable prayer is not just a set of words to be mouthed as a ritual but rather, is a prayer that connects the eternal with the present, giving hope for the future. It was always meant to be an inspiration for future living, the things that are to come.

The Lord's Prayer is bursting at the seams with theological truths and indicators to the nature of God and His kingdom that can't be squeezed into a little box, brought out Sunday by Sunday and put away again. God is always our Father, day-by-day, night-by-night from now through all of eternity. His power and glory have always been in existence and have never dimmed for a second. He has always provided for His children and He always will. Do you see? It is a prayer for now, but it is a prayer for what is to come.

As we pray it again here, take time to consider these things.

Our Father in heaven
Hallowed be Your name
Your kingdom come
Your will be done
On earth as it is in heaven
Give us this day our daily bread
And forgive us our debts
As we forgive our debtors
And do not lead us into temptation
But deliver us from the evil one
For Yours is the kingdom and the power and the glory forever.
Amen. Matthew 6:9-13

Time to Reflect

- What new things have you discovered about The Lord's Prayer during the reading of this book?
- Are you ready to delve deeper into understanding how to live your life to adapt to the principles of this unique prayer?
- How will you begin to do that?
- Do you need help in areas of your life where you struggle with temptation and have not known how to overcome it?
- Do you doubt that God will provide for you throughout your life?
- How has studying The Lord's Prayer in more depth encouraged you to see God differently?

Meditate

There is no time like the present to get right with God. So right now, wherever you are, begin to tell Him you are ready and open for Him to come and change you. You may need washing clean from sinful behaviour that has stuck to your soul and made you feel dirty. You may need to repent of false judgments you have made against a person or you may be struggling with unforgiveness towards someone. Maybe people have spoken lies about you and you are feeling angry and misrepresented. Whatever the issue, God wants you to be free! Jesus died to release you from the things that come along to sap your energy and make you feel like life is too tough. Let's pray.

"Father, I come to you now and acknowledge my need of You. I can't do any of this on my own. I have prayed your prayer and I understand the truths in it more than I did, and it has made me realize just how much I thought I knew, but I don't! I'm ready to let you in to my heart and change me some more so I can embrace You with more eagerness than I have done before. I want to say 'Yes and amen' to You and all the wonderful things about You that this prayer highlights to me. I want to say 'so be it' to victory over temptation in the areas You know about. I want to say sorry for the times I have doubted Your provision for my life when year by year I can testify to how You have looked after me. I want to tell You how hard it is to forgive the people You have seen hurt me, but because You have forgiven me, I want to forgive them. I'm also really hungry for some glory encounters which take me from a mediocre Christian life to one characterized by the power of Your kingdom in me and around me. If there is a heaven full of promises I want them now! I love You Lord, even when I don't feel good enough; I still love You and know You love me. Set me back on track and over my life will You please now shout a loud 'AMEN!' Thank you, my Father. Amen."

About the Author

Rt Revd Dr David Carr is the Senior Pastor at Renewal Christian Centre, Solihull.

A writer, broadcaster and pastor, David travels extensively across the globe, sharing his vision and ministering in some of the most deprived areas of the world with missions aimed at alleviating the struggle of orphans, disabled children and people whose lives have been devastated by disaster.

Closer to home, he founded a mission to feed families within his local region who found themselves in difficulty (now termed "the fourth emergency service" by Solihull's Mayor) and he is patron of the Gateway Foundation – a charity to support and mentor recovering drug addicts, alcoholics and ex-offenders.

In 2009 David established The Order of St Leonard as a result of his vision to provide an Order of Convergence – allowing members of a wide spectrum of Christian denominations to gather together to develop their walk with God.

In July 2009, he was consecrated as Bishop and Abbot of the Order of St Leonard at Wren's Cathedral, which is now the official seat of the Bishop of Wroxall Abbey. The Order of St Leonard has grown exponentially since its foundation in 2009. Members from many differing denominations and streams are joining and working together with the common purpose of bringing the Word of Jesus Christ to the world; supporting the disadvantaged, liberating those captives of physical, spiritual and emotional bonds, and loving one another, and our communities.